C000212816

Steve Porter.
June 1983.

Boatfishing for Trout

BOATFISHING
=FOR TROUT=

STEVE PARTON

London
GEORGE ALLEN & UNWIN
Boston   Sydney

© Steve Parton, 1983.
This book is copyright under the Berne Convention. No reproduction
without permission. All rights reserved.

**George Allen & Unwin (Publishers) Ltd,
40 Museum Street, London WC1A 1LU, UK**

George Allen & Unwin (Publishers) Ltd,
Park Lane, Hemel Hempstead, Herts HP2 4TE, UK

Allen & Unwin Inc.,
9 Winchester Terrace, Winchester, Mass 01890, USA

George Allen & Unwin Australia Pty Ltd,
8 Napier Street, North Sydney, NSW 2060, Australia

First published 1983

British Library Cataloguing in Publication Data

Parton, Steve
  Boatfishing for trout.
1. Trout fishing
I. Title
799.1'755   SH6887
ISBN 0–04–799016–3

Set in 10 on 12 point Palatino by Nene Phototypesetters, Northampton
and printed in Great Britain by William Clowes Limited,
Beccles and London

Contents

List of Illustrations

Plates

Figures

Acknowledgements

The author wishes to thank a number of fishermen and friends for help in the writing of this book. Amongst the more notable are John Wilshaw, Editor of *Trout Fisherman* and his staff who gave unstintingly of their time, trouble and copyright. Tom Saville and Jim Clements read the drafts and pointed out omissions. The photographs are the work of Bob Carnill, Dave Greaves, John Wilshaw and Terry Griffiths. Janet Dolby transformed the author's sketches into the diagrams, a voyage of exploration for a non-fisherwoman. Karen Von Klosst-Dohna, Janet Briggs and Linda Smith were able to decipher the author's appalling handwriting through three drafts and type up the manuscripts; it is hoped that they will make a satisfactory recovery.

Others who helped were Chris Aylett of Gladding, Norman Bexon, Messrs Fibatube, Bob Church, Geoff Davis, Cecil Dobney, Tommy Graham, Tony Knight, Pete Tasker and fellow bailiffs at Rutland Water; and last but not least Eric Watson and Gordon Edwards.

Introduction

It has become a rarity to have the chance to fish the banks of a major stillwater in the ways that were traditional only twenty years ago. The increase in fishing pressure has seen the decline of the fisherman who quietly worked his way along the bank taking his fish. Bankfishing has now become a heron-like occupation for most fishermen, who seem willing to take rooted positions for the entire day, and who demonstrate, sometimes aggressively, all the behaviour patterns associated with the territorial imperative, concerning the water within their casting range. Bankfishing, being closely related to the fishing of known hotspots, has as much to do nowadays with the race for possession of such a hotspot, as with actual fishing skills.

The boat is really the refuge of the free spirits amongst stillwater fishermen. It provides the chance for the enterprising to seek out their quarry without being unduly squeezed for elbow room. Not only that, but the scope offered by the boat is much greater in terms of fishing methods and tactics. While there is at times a close parallel between bankside and boatfishing techniques, boatfishing is a fundamentally different sport requiring different patterns of thought and approach in order to take trout.

The first is in the time of day. By boatfishing, trout can be caught right through the day during most of the season. This is not the case with bankfishing which is essentially an early morning and late evening occupation. As such the latter is well suited to locals who are able to fish for short periods of time and then go home or to work during the less productive hours of full daylight; it is not suited at all to fishermen with restricted leisure opportunities due to work, family and travel pressures. Generally, boatfishing will produce more fish at the end of the day than bankfishing, at a ratio, in my experience, of around 3:1. An important consideration to fishermen who like to catch fish instead of enjoying the beauties of nature, which is often all there is to appreciate in a day of bankfishing.

The second major difference is that the contest between fisherman and fish becomes much more immediate. Using a boat removes the excuse that the fish were 'out of range'; there is no excuse for failure when boatfishing.

Naturally, fishery managements are well aware of the general effectiveness of boatfishing and, as a result, charge a heavy additional premium for the hire of boats. The present cost of putting two men afloat for a day on Rutland Water amounts to rather more than a quarter of the net weekly wage of the average Briton. The severity of the cost burden not only adds fuel to the intensity of the contest between fisherman and fish but also emphasises the need for a much more planned and organised approach than is generally required for bankfishing.

The culminating result of these pressures upon the boat fisherman to catch fish has been to force the pace of technical development. The last two decades have seen more radical changes in boatfishing techniques than in any other form of stillwater fly fishing. The sport has now become so diverse in methodology that it is difficult for a single work upon the subject to do little more than touch upon the major approaches and give the fisherman a hint of the many ways of taking trout from a boat.

With this apology, I have attempted to lead the reader: firstly, through the strategy behind boatfishing; secondly, through the basic methods and tactics; and finally, through the ways of applying those methods to produce the results that one desires, whatever they may be.

It should be pointed out that there is little chance of a fisherman becoming adept in all of the methods outlined without at least a decade of practice. Despite having boatfished some 400 days in the last decade and seen more than 5,000 fish come into the boats that I have fished from, I class myself as a beginner at the sport. There is so much to learn, to think out, and to develop, so many questions that haven't even been asked yet; it may take me a lifetime to attain a reasonable standard of performance. Hopefully, this book will save you some of the years that I have already spent learning and much of the money that you would waste in repeating the many mistakes that I have made in that time.

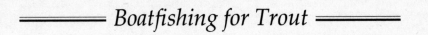

Boatfishing for Trout

1 *Boatfishing Strategy*

Objectives

The most useful exercise the prospective boat fisher can undertake, before all else, is to define what he or she wants to get out of fishing. Only when one has an objective can one begin to take the logical steps towards achieving it.

There are many different personal objectives possible in purely fishing terms. They may range from the modest desire of the beginner to catch just one fish in the day to the ultimate desire of the master to take the eight largest fish in the water in as many casts. There are many other variations, some may pursue specimen fish, some may play the numbers game, competition fishermen may seek to maximise the total weight caught. At the end of the day, however, all these desires can usually be satisfied by catching a reasonable number of adequately-sized fish.

This simple objective is by no means easy to achieve consistently. Frequently, the situation is exacerbated by the existence of fishery rules which seem designed to thwart the consistent capture of fish.

It is a feature of boatfishing on large and substantially unrestricted fisheries that on 95 days out of 100 it is possible to return to the boathouse with a limit of reasonable fish, no matter how vile and adverse conditions may have been. It is certain that many different methods and their associated tactics will have to be used to produce consistent catches right through the season. Specific methods and tactics are appropriate only to the set of conditions that they were developed to deal with. It is, for example, just as pointless to fish for rising trout with a leadcored shooting head as it is to fish for deeply-lying bottom feeders with a floating line.

Choice of fishery: restrictions

Ignorance of this cardinal feature of stillwater boating has led, sadly in my view, to many fisheries establishing rules which prohibit the use of several of the methods outlined in the purely technical chapters of this book. The restriction of methods has the effect of increasing the amount of days upon which it is not possible to take a reasonable limit, due to the inappropriateness of permitted methods in certain weather conditions or times of the year.

Interestingly, the long-term result of such restrictions is not a wholesale reduction of numbers of fish taken, it is extreme inconsistency in the fishing from one day to the next. The dearth experienced during unfavourable conditions is followed by the boom when conditions favour the allowed methods. Fishermen on a restricted-method water have to face the prospect that they will spend a considerable proportion of the season wasting their efforts and the rest of the time having relatively easy fishing.

The problems associated with such tactical restrictions on certain waters present the prospective boat fisherman with considerable problems in selecting where and how to fish.

The complete beginner is advised to make his way to a restricted-method fishery and to spend a couple of seasons in getting to grips with the particular techniques allowed. As his expertise increases there will be occasions when good bags of fish will be caught; but inconsistency will remain. Having gained a grip of a few techniques, the individual is then much better prepared to move on to a larger multi-method fishery to broaden his knowledge.

An experienced fisherman who voluntarily opts to restrict his approach solely to one or two methods has no right to complain when fellow fishermen apply alternative legitimate methods and catch more fish. Fly fishing is a sport curiously afflicted by jealousy; few experienced fishermen seem able to admit that they are in any way deficient performers. In fishing, as in every other field sport, there are wide differences in ability between individuals; the best fishermen catch fish more consistently, no matter what restrictions are placed upon them.

I am strongly in favour of waters which allow multi-method fly fishing, as I know that by using the full range of techniques I can catch fish most of the time if I fish well. I do not require easy fishing, I prefer it hard but fair and do not grumble much when the fish beat me. My objective for the boat is to take a reasonable double limit on every trip; I get thwarted very frequently, I am glad to say.

If your primary objective is the same as mine, I recommend that you seek to master all the methods outlined and then develop either new methods or further tactical variations to fill in the gaps in your expertise.

Choice of fishery: stocking patterns

A further factor complicates the decision of where to fish: the stocking policy of the particular water.

Fishermen may well be the most irrational consumers at large in the United Kingdom; they seem to have a blind faith in the ability of fishery managers to guarantee a reasonable head of fish in the water. Bitter experience has taught me that this is frequently not the case. If there are no fish in the water, it doesn't matter whether you are an expert or a beginner, you will not catch them.

No shrewd fisherman should contemplate picking a water for a season's fishing without having as full a knowledge as possible of its stocking policy. Not only is the seasonal stocking policy of importance in this respect, but also the likely overwintered head of fish must be taken into account. Fishery managers tend to make fairly bold assertions as to the proportion of the previous season's uncaught fish that have survived the winter. It is safe only to assume that half the uncaught brown trout still survive, and, with certain notable exceptions including Grafham, rainbows should be considered to have perished entirely (though a few will survive a mild winter, a very few only).

If faced with the fairly common situation of a complete lack of pre-season stocking information, the only recourse a fisherman has is to join an Association or Club and then to agitate until the fishery management begins to show more commercial sense and openness in the matter. Either that, or vote with the feet.

It is a great mistake to think that one will catch more fish by chasing the catch returns around the various waters – quite apart from the practical difficulties in attempting to book up boats; and to organise a day's fishing on an *ad hoc* basis there are the added disadvantages of inadequate local knowledge and the increased expense of fishing without a season ticket.

Local knowledge: underwater geography

Many factors determine what makes an expert fisherman, not least is the quality of his local knowledge of a water. Good local knowledge will produce fish when others are doing very badly indeed; poor local knowledge can ensure a blank in times of plenty. Most of the larger fisheries cannot be 'learned' in one season alone due to the very considerable weather and moonphase variations that disrupt, advance or delay the pattern of fishing from year to year. I have fished Rutland Water since it opened and am only just beginning to realise that water's potential and even then I do not know even half the reservoir nearly as well as I ought. Smaller waters are easier to learn.

How does one find out about a water? The best first step is to obtain a decent map of the area of the pre-flooding vintage. Ideally, such a map should be of the 25 inches to the mile variety and highly detailed, down to footpaths, headlands and field troughs. Using a post-flooding map it is then easy to transfer the outline onto your large map and gain, at a stroke, an immediate wealth of local knowledge of the water of the theoretical sort. Theoretical, because it is still necessary to conduct a series of experiments to confirm the indications on the map.

These experiments should be carried out in a variety of ways: plumbing with a lead weight and metered string, deep drift fishing, anchor fishing and echo sounding. All these experiments must be related very precisely to visible topographical features around the shore so that they can be etched into the memory. Beware of the inherent danger of using yacht racing buoys in this regard – yachts-men are in the habit of moving them! So, if you do use buoys, as I do, recheck their positions from time to time.

The objective in using maps and in doing the various experiments is twofold: firstly, to establish mentally a clear picture of the bottom profile and, secondly, to establish which drift lines are likely to produce the best results, on which winds, at which depth and at which time of year.

Using the Echo Sounder is one major way of acquiring a great deal of knowledge of the bottom profile in a very short time. The one I use is the Seafarer Mark 3 with dial indicator. There are other types on the market, some ludicrously expensive, I do not recommend them! One should not attempt to use the Echo Sounder to locate fish. It certainly will locate fish but, alas, they will not necessarily be trout and your efforts at catching roach or bream with lures are likely to be as unproductive as mine have been over the years. (I once caught a roach of 2 lb. 3 oz. at Eyebrook with a Rasputin over deep water and a 6 lb. bream at Grafham with a Zuluka on the lead – good fish but only two in ten years.) And God help you if your machine finds you a shoal of hungry jack pike.

The real use of the Echo Sounder is in locating bottom features that may hold fish for much of the season. Shoaling water is critically important, particularly the detail of the falls from shallow to deep water around the shoal edge. Old stream beds, as at Eyebrook and in the Rutland arms, are also well worth knowing about. Drowned roads, old hedge and ditch lines, demolished structures and old forestry plantations, all must be fixed in your mental picture of the bottom.

The plotting of inshore deeps is also well worth undertaking as such water is often highly productive. This water is subject to exaggerated bottom contours. One has to establish, for example, the location of the 30-foot line in relation to a shore that may be only 30 yards away. Without such knowledge, it is impossible to straight-line drift fish such a bottom accurately as one has to know when to throw shallow or when to pay out line and fish deeper so as to drop the fly as close to the bottom as possible. Intimate knowledge of the bottom profile not only catches fish, it has an additional advantage in that you don't lose your flies quite as often!

Local knowledge: feeding patterns

All stillwaters differ in terms of their food populations. Immediate examples that spring to mind are the red buzzers of Chew, the green and clarets of Pitsford, the red-goes-gingers of Eyebrook and the May hatching olives of Grafham and Rutland. Some waters have green buzzers, others have the brown – all waters are different.

It is as well to keep a note of the dates and times of the emergent insect populations and, more importantly, the food forms that your captures have been indulging themselves on. To this end, one must observe what is coming off and falling onto the water; always carry a marrow scoop to examine the stomach contents of your catch.

The pattern of fry emergence and the feeding behaviour of trout in relation to it is also worthy of note. If you know that your water starts producing pinfry in late June you will not be deceived the following year by the apparently furious rise to fly, that is, in fact, a rise to masses of tiny fishes.

The same rise peculiarities observed with the emergence of pinfry can apply at different times of year to emergences of snails, shrimps, drone flies, leeches and, wickedest of all, surfaced daphnia in late May. Careful records of the likely times of such happenings can transform a potential disaster into a beanfeast.

Naturally, the weather can advance, retard or eliminate any of these emergence cycles in any one year. It is very annoying to be itching to have a go at, say, dapping 'daddies' only to be greeted by a fortnight of calm weather in early September. These things frequently happen and all one can do is smile and put the gear away until next season.

Given the time and the opportunity, the last major way for the boat specialist to further his knowledge of his local water is to fish it from the bank. In addition, bankside nymphing teaches one all the pure fishing technique one will ever require for fishing square-on at anchor, besides offering one invaluable practice in careful, accurate casting.

It might be supposed that all one has to do to catch fish from a boat is basically to duplicate bankside tactics, particularly with regard to the selection of imitative flies. This is not the case at all; it is, for example, rare for the small buzzer patterns beloved of the evening bank fisherman to be nearly so effective when applied at the same time of night from an offshore boat.

Bankfishing is concerned with shallow water, boatfishing takes place over deeper water and there are very significant differences in the chironomid populations between the two habitats, particularly in terms of the timing of emergences.

It should also be remembered that the really deadly time for bankfishing is the last half hour of light – well after the boats have set off back to their moorings. At that time the fish tend to be specialising in picking off hatching and laying adult flies; duplicating half light tactics in full light conditions will contribute little to your success.

With sedges, as opposed to buzzers, the comparison is very much closer. Evening sedge patterns from the bank are pretty much the same as evening boat patterns. It frequently pays to use slightly larger sedge pupae imitations from the boat than from the bank at evening; offshore sedge takers are that little bit more incautious.

But the real value of bankfishing to the boat angler is in establishing when and where fish are running inshore. At Rutland, there is a movement of fish into the shallows, sometime in late May or early June. This happening signals two things to the boat fisherman, firstly, that it is time to use small fly tactics through the day and, secondly, that the South Arm Nature Reserve is well worth fishing at anchor.

Morning and evening inshore runs from deepwaters indicate that the fish are holding deep in the daytime. This is particularly useful in the latter part of the season, as it pays to fish deep just offshore from those parts of the bank where the bigger brownies are being taken, either drifting or at anchor. Another way of furthering your local knowledge, by operating an information net with other fishermen, is dealt with later.

Suffice it to say that the more you know about your home waters, the more fish you will catch as a result.

The team approach

Boatfishing is the natural province of the two-man team. Many waters will not allow a fisherman to take a boat out on his own. The practice of fishing with three men in a boat is one that I rarely indulge in as it is overcrowded and can be dangerous; it also restricts many of the tactical options open to the two-man crew.

It takes quite a long time for an effective team to be formed, the knocking off of the rough edges, the joint boatmanship, and the developed anticipation of each other's moves and intentions, all take time. It is quite essential for fishermen to operate in long-term partnership from the boats – there really is no other way. I am unaware of any highly successful fisherman who operates with a continuous change of partners. The consistent fish-takers that I know, irrespective of their fishing styles, always operate in partnership. Often the dissolution of a successful fishing partnership results in the decline of both partners as effective fishermen. The phenomenon of synergy plays a large part in this, with a fishing team one plus one equals a great deal more than the sum of the two individual talents.

The team approach is crucial to effective fishing as the general rule with all styles is for each to operate around the other, running complementary experiments in terms of fly, depth and presentation. Each partner invariably has different skills and this has to be made use of in the team approach. Some years ago, I fished a season with Ron Burgin. He had a great fondness for fishing the leadline, whenever we 'lost' the fish I could be certain that Ron would turn to leading, thus ensuring that the nether depths were thoroughly covered. I would then fish the strata above so that when he struck fish I could put the lead on, and when I hit the fish he could change to my tactics. A wide diversity of talent is no bad thing; probably the most effective present day team is that currently formed by Dick Shrive and Frank Cutler, a deep lure specialist and a small fly expert respectively.

Fishing partnerships have to be composed of compatible individuals to be successful, rather like a marriage. Despite recent improvements in design, a fishing boat is still a very small place if neither of you get on with each other; it is as well to remember that it is considerably smaller than a two-man cell in one of Her Majesty's prisons. Your partner must be chosen with great care as an injudicious selection can be disastrous.

In a two-man team there is little point in competing against one another. There are very many ways, for instance, in which the helmsman of the boat is able to influence the movement of the boat to such an extent as to render his partner's efforts fairly ineffectual. Over the years, my experiences with partners of the competitive type have been sufficiently unpleasant for me to be able to state that I will never again get into a boat with a fisherman unwilling to share the day in the fullest sense of the word. As far as I am concerned, two fishermen in one boat competing against each other represents a perversion afloat.

A good partner knows when to talk and when to stay silent, when to suggest a change and when to have a brilliant idea; if you find a good partner stick to him (or her) like glue, they are generally irreplaceable.

Planning

Before setting out to fish from a boat, the fisherman should have recruited a partner and together they should have jointly formulated a fairly detailed series of plans concerning the choice of water and the ways in which they are to gather local knowledge of that water. It may seem rather obvious to mention it, but coupled with the decision to fish a particular water goes the simple problem of booking a boat and paying for it. All waters have different administrative systems, some require booking a month in advance, some require booking a season in advance. Failure to find out about the systems in operation at the water of your choice could cost the first two months of boat bookings in the season and a great deal of annoyance to boot.

To develop a basic tactical plan for the season is no bad idea. In this regard, it is essential to establish a record system so organised as to be of use in future planning. Most fishermen who keep records do so in the form of a diary or game-log, very pleasant to read, remember and reflect upon in the close season but fairly useless as a systematic aide memoire for the seasons to come. I keep all my records on individual cards in a small card file. I arrange them in month and date order, independent of year. At a glance I can survey, for example, Maytime fishing for the last five years, a simple record of over 60 boat trips, very quick to scan.

Before going boatfishing, therefore, a considerable amount of groundwork must be undertaken to give one a fair chance of success. Summing it up, one must plan for the season to come in many ways: fishing objectives, where to fish, the amassing of local knowledge, the recruitment of a partner and the processing of information.

Boatfishing is as subject to analysis and planning as any other human activity. In this context never forget what Confucius actually did say, 'If you don't know which way you are going, any road will do.' This attitude is all too common amongst boat fishermen, it is entirely inadequate if you intend to catch fish consistently.

2 *Fishing from anchor*

Anchor fishing, like bankfishing, separates naturally into two distinct styles. Square-on anchoring relates closely to bankside nymphing techniques and nose-down anchoring relates equally closely to fishing with the lure. Before moving onto a detailed analysis of these separate styles, it is necessary to outline the features common to both: the hardware essential for controlling the boat.

Hardware

Different waters, boats and weather conditions present different problems in anchoring, none of them confuse the main point: an anchor must be sufficient to hold a boat steady without dragging from the combined pressures of wind, wave and current. One can get into situations in which it is neither reasonable nor safe to contemplate anchoring at all! A force 6 wind and a mile long reach of water can generate very impressive waves indeed, and even if you have gear that can hold the boat in such conditions it is likely that you will be unable to retrieve the anchor when you do decide to move, it would need to weigh about a hundredweight.

I have one main rig for anchoring which will deal with most likely conditions: it is a two-part rig consisting of a 3-pronged grappling iron (10 inches between prongs) weighing 5 lb., shackled to 30 feet of chain which itself weighs some 25 lb. This formidable assemblage is securely knotted to 150 feet of ½-inch diameter polypropylene rope. Always use polypropylene rope as it is buoyant and when one makes the inevitable mistake and the whole lot goes over the side, no lasting harm is done. One simply rows round, spots it floating and picks it up again.

The chain is essential as it changes the direction of the pull upon the anchor as shown in the diagram (Fig. 1).

An anchor without a decent length of chain is very ineffective

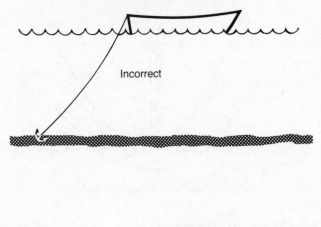

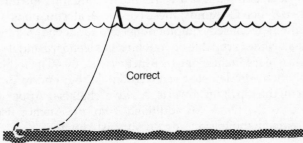

Fig. 1 Using a chain to create an horizontal pull on the anchor

indeed. It will not hold the bottom in a 6-inch wave, let alone a 3-foot one. I always carry two identical rigs of this type.

Additionally, I have a third anchor designed specifically to hold the very light boats at Foremark Reservoir over immense depths – it is no joke pulling up 30 lb. of anchor and chain out of 100 feet of water. This anchor (Fig. 2) weighs around 10 lb. and the points must be very sharp indeed. It is attached directly to 200 feet of 1/4-inch diameter buoyant terylene line.

This rig would not hold a Rutland boat over 20 feet of water but at Foremark with light boats, small waves and the cushioning effect of around 150 feet of thin, stretchy rope it will hold in up to 120 feet.

I carry my ropes on large wooden stringers, each stringer has a hole drilled in it for the end of the rope to pass through, a knot is then tied to secure it. The anchors and chains live in their own stout canvas sacks.

Anchors must be firmly fixed to the boat: this is best achieved by

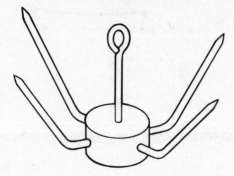

Fig. 2   Foremark deepwater anchor

clamping a G-cramp to the thwarts and leading the rope through it; I carry two 6-inch G-cramps, these cope with all situations.

The other specialised equipment needed for anchor fishing is the plank-seat. Mine is capable of doubling as a leeboard and it consists of a plank 6 feet 6 inches long by 8 inches wide by ½ inch thick with a 1×1×8 inch wooden stop screwed onto either end to prevent it slipping off the top of the thwarts. A swivel chair (see Appendix) can be bolted to the plank for additional comfort. Anchor fishing is always seated fishing; standing up puts fish down.

Square-on anchoring

In order to present small flies effectively it is essential that the boat is anchored as solidly as possible. This requirement precludes the use of one anchor alone. If a boat is anchored centrally with just one anchor it will yaw from side to side.

If you wish to fish very slowly using deep nymphs and a figure of eight retrieve, or if the fish are taking the fly on the drop, a yawing boat greatly limits effectiveness. It is surprising just how far a boat will yaw even in the shallowest upwind water with the gentlest breeze blowing and the shortest length of rope out.

The answer is to use an anchor at either end of the boat; this doubles the inconvenience, but probably quadruples the effectiveness. In order to anchor in this manner the procedure to be adopted is as follows. Approach the spot you wish to anchor over on a line about 15 yards upwind and coming in from the side. Every movement must be made as quietly as possible to avoid disturbance. The engine is cut and the man at the stern lowers his anchor and pays out rope until the boat stops, as soon as the boat has stopped the bow man drops his anchor and exactly the same amount of rope over the upwind side of the boat (the ropes should be marked at equal intervals to assist in this manoeuvre). Both parties then secure their respective ropes and within a minute or so the boat will drift quietly down the wind until it reaches the equilibrium point between both anchor ropes.

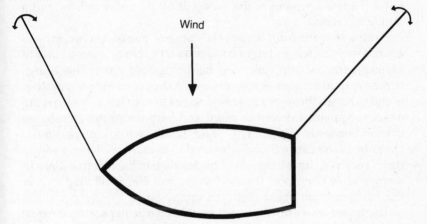

Wind

Fig. 3 Square-on anchoring: anchor attachment positions for maximum stability and minimum yaw

To fish effectively some attention must be paid to the way in which the boat is organised. Firstly, the net must be to hand so that either of you can grab it swiftly and easily; it should have an extending handle if you propose to use a long leader, if it hasn't got one you will have very considerable problems in netting a fish that has taken your point fly (unless, of course, your rod is about 20 feet long). Netting drill is very important if you want to maximise your chances and maintain some harmony within the boat. One iron rule has to be followed: as soon as a fish is hooked the other fisherman must get his tackle out of the way in order to net the fish. A good reliable netsman is the most valuable of fishing companions, even if he never catches a damned thing himself and has to be given half the fish at the end of the day. In this regard a large net helps greatly, the bigger the better. It is an advantage to have the frame bent at 15° to the handle, as this increases the effective area.

The clutter in the bottom of the boat must be reduced to an absolute minimum. Fishing tackle, bags, spare rods, jackets etc., all seem to be infested with projecting snags that catch your line, disrupt your concentration and prevent you from fishing smoothly and without strain. The easiest way I know of minimising snags is to carry a couple of plastic sacks and to put everything you aren't using into them and then stow it all behind you in a tidy manner.

Spare rods should be stacked well out of the way and on no account left to project above or outside the thwarts. Likewise for the net – if anything projects the flies will hit it sooner or later and a tangle will result.

Fishing over the front has special dangers; one of you (unless you are respectively left and right handers) will have the onerous task of casting with his companion on his immediate right. This brings certain responsibilities as it is very easy to forget where your partner is and to have a throw at a riser well across to your left. I recall having a size 6 Appetizer driven in point and barb under my chin by an over-enthusiastic friend. The wind, as it swirls, causes similar hazards: partnering a friend who tended to cast a bit flat one windy day, I received the full benefit of his leadline in the face five times in a remarkable afternoon; it raised weals, just like a bullwhip. Never fish leadcore from a boat anchored square-on.

The better caster must be assigned this particular seat in the boat and his partner should make a point of wearing a pair of glasses of some kind and a substantial hat (yes, you can be wounded on both the forward and back casts). Years ago, when I used to fish with Ron Burgin at Eyebrook, I always fished in the left hand seat and I made a point of apologising for hitting him before we ever got into the boat. He used to fish with sunglasses on and hood up in anything windier than force 2 Beaufort, as a matter of course!

Tackle for square-on fishing

For this style of fishing, which is basically bankside nymphing taken offshore, the right tackle to use is bankside nymphing tackle. I use a 10-foot Lamiglas blank rated AFTM 6/7 that actually takes DT 5 and 6 lines (the 6 for the windier days) held on a wide drum Fishhawk or Speedex multiplier. As a matter of course I use Cortland lines in the prettier colours such as fluorescent red or green; I like to fish with lines that I can see well out, they don't seem to put the fish down much.

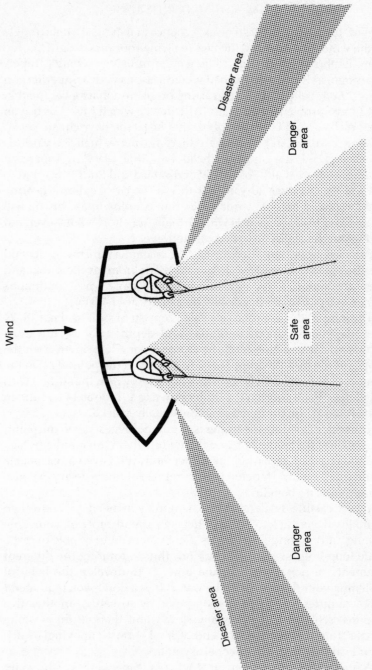

Fig. 4   Safe and unsafe sectors

With this style, there isn't much chance of fishing at a sharp angle to the wind and allowing the flies to swing round on a tight line, so there is no real advantage to be gained in using a Double Taper. Years ago, at Eyebrook, I fished whole seasons with a Superlite and a no. 7 Longbelly and had no casting problems whatsoever, neither did I have problems with a no. 7 FT floater which I used to use on Dick Walker's old Grafham Ghost that he let me have cheap.

Long casting isn't required either, no more than 25 yards is necessary and the shooting head has little place in square-on fishing. Unless, that is, one is old or disabled and finds it an effort to get the fly out over 20 yards. If this is the case, splice a floating shooting head onto 25 yards of floating running line. This rig will enable you to cast 25 yards with virtually no effort whatsoever and still retain the ability to hand twist retrieve.

Far more important than the casting machinery are the leader and the droppers. My leaders are always made from level monofil and they are almost invariably heavy. These days I use continuous Tynex in 5 or 6 lb. BS (it actually breaks dry at 11–13 lb.).

The long leader approach is vital to consistent success. I use 18–24 feet, depending upon conditions and depth. I follow the Cove dictats on construction with the top dropper 3 feet down from the loop and the middle dropper 6–7 feet up from the point fly. On the rarer occasions when it is necessary to fish very near the surface with small flies, I will shorten the leader down to as little as 14 feet and in that situation the droppers are more equally spaced.

The trick in loading the leader is to put the biggest fly on the point, the smallest fly on the bob and the middle fly in the middle (which has the effect of 'tapering' the leader anyway). Given a reasonable standard of casting, tapered leaders represent unnecessary expense and provide no benefit.

When casting leaders of this length, you need to know two wrinkles if you are to ensure that you spend most of your time fishing and not undoing tangles. First you need to be able to cast a wide loop both in front and behind, thus separating the different segments of aerialised line; the other is to develop the habit of watching your flies fall onto the water. If you don't, you may spend three minutes waiting for your point fly to settle, another five minutes retrieving exceptionally slowly and then lift an amazing tangle from the water at the end of it all – most annoying! Watch your leader unfold, whatever else you do.

A further key rule is to ensure that your leader lands on the water fully extended. This applies as much even to leadlining as to anchored small-fly fishing.

The final accessories required to fish effectively in this style may sound obvious but are very often forgotten in practice: a floatant and a degreaser for your line and leader. There is only one brand of floatant really worth bothering with, Mucilin, in the red tins; for a degreaser take some mud off the bank, it's very cheap, and just as good as the proprietary stuffs (which are usually made up by mixing Fuller's Earth with Fairy Liquid). I have at least six tins of Mucilin distributed amongst tackle bags, coats and waistcoat. Occasionally, I manage to find one to use!

Where and when

The basic requirement for square-on fishing to be profitable is to locate a spot in shallow water into which fish will run (and feed) in the daytime. The style is only really suitable in water up to 15 feet deep and, ideally, should not be adopted for water deeper than 10–12 feet. A useful guideline is to poke your rod into the water over the front of the boat, if you get your elbow wet before you encounter the bottom, then think about moving.

The best shallows available tend to be in Nature Reserves and Bird Sanctuaries where there are no bank fishermen to disturb the fish, and in these situations it usually pays to anchor the boat as close to the bank as possible without infringing the fishery rules.

Shoal water is often a very good bet as well: Grafham has the S. Buoy shoals, Rutland the South Arm Island shoals and Draycote the Toft shoals and shallows, there are others elsewhere.

One interesting lesson I learned years ago at Eyebrook was to make use of bank fishermen. These obliging individuals often encouraged the fish to feed about 50 yards out from the bank in the daytime, frequently it paid to anchor the boat just out of their casting range. This wheeze undoubtedly works elsewhere.

The style pays best when you are anchored close to the bank from which the wind is blowing, particularly when terrestrial insects are being blown onto the water. As a technique, it is generally of little use when applied near a lee shore in any sizeable wind or wave. Occasionally, it is possible to get into a favourable position off a semi-lee shore where a running line for fish develops around a headland or promontary (see Fig. 5).

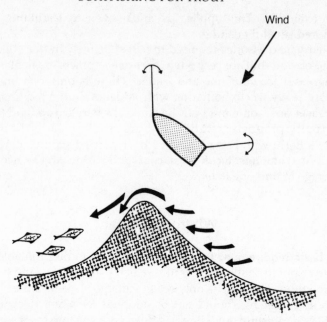

Fig. 5 Anchoring off a leeshore promontory to take advantage of wind
generated currents

The trick here is to fish just wide of the disturbed water and in
such a position that you can cast onshore into the spots that a bank
fisherman cannot cover due to the prevailing wind.

Early on in the season fish tend to do a great deal of their daytime
feeding at some considerable depth, coming into the shallows only
in the mornings and evenings. The right time to anchor square-on is
between June and September. The tail of the season sees the demise
of small-fly fishing from the boats. In the mid season, big winds and
flat calms also tend to limit the effectiveness of square-on fishing as
well. Nice muggy grey days or pleasant sunny days with a fair
amount of cumulus cloud cover are the ones you really want.

Tactics

Tactics are a two-man concern; it is essential that partners work
around each other until a taking method is found. There is little
point in flogging away in one style with the same flies on for hour

after hour and catching nothing. Patience is not a fishing virtue, it generates blank days. What needs to be cultivated is organised impatience. The following basic tactics can be worked through quite systematically until a taking method is found.

Deep nymphing

The basic object of deep nymph fishing is to present the point fly either just above the bottom if there is weed, or hard along the bottom if it is clean. The first problem to sort out is how to get the point fly down deep. The major methods are:

(1) Using a floating line, long leader and a heavy, but unleaded, point fly like a size 8 or 6 Cove's Pheasant Tail, one casts out and waits while the flies settle. This may take two to three minutes to happen and, on occasion, generates a take on the fall so you should hold on and watch very closely as the flies sink.

The retrieve is made by hand twisting and must be sufficiently slow as to keep the fly very near the bottom. I retrieve with my rod tip within 3 inches of the surface, pointing straight down the line. The latter should not pass round the index finger of the rod hand because you get a smoother retrieve if you learn to fish and strike with the line going straight into your retrieving hand from the butt ring.

Very often you will see the tip of your line (which should be greased for the end 6 feet) disappear into a little hole in the water – strike sideways, never by lifting the rod, and you won't miss.

Most takes tend to be felt rather than seen, you either have them or you don't. One kind to be wary of is the tap take, in which you can feel a fish pinching the fly very gently – don't strike until the fish has taken hold. It is always terribly hard to restrain yourself.

(2) A faster way of getting the fly down is to cast out and then to pay or shake out two or three extra yards. This causes the point fly to fall vertically through the water, without the effect of water resistance on the full length of the leader braking its fall. Use this approach if the taking fish are on the bottom and are not taking the fly on the drop.

(3) Using a leaded point fly will enable you to engage in sink and draw fishing. Retrieve by pulling a foot or so of line in at a time with the line going round the index finger of the right hand and either feeling for the take or watching the loop of line between the tip of the rod and the surface.

In deep nymphing, the droppers are usually irrelevant to the main business which is to present a large fly representing Caddis, Buzzer, Leech, Damsel nymph, Alder or Dytiscus beetle along the bottom in a natural manner. This does not mean that you should neglect them. Put on flies that represent other food forms appropriate to the area and the time of year. Buzzers are often a good bet, perhaps a size 10 on the second dropper and a size 12 on the bob. The main colours I choose are olives, buffs, browns and blacks. Some buzzers have the nasty habit of being a different colour in the air from that which the pupae were in the water; ginger can be red, green olive can be claret and black can be grey. You should not only examine what is hatching off, but also use your marrow scoop on the victims.

(4) Paternoster nymphing is sometimes useful in water containing shrimps. The point fly, which should be leaded, is fished dragging in the weed and the shrimp pattern will fish just over it if rigged on a long dropper about 3 feet above the point fly.

When shrimps abound, two patterns are required: a large, pale Gold Ribbed Hare's Ear nymph tied on a wide gape hook to suggest shrimpiness, and the Clement's Crustacean to deal with the orange coloured mating shrimp. (This latter pattern can be deadly for big brownies applied off the bank on evenings when the shrimp feed is on.)

Midwater and induction fishing

Sooner or later you will discover fish feeding in the midwater and these fish are usually best taken on a pull retrieve as they tend to be feeding on relatively active food forms such as pupae rising towards the surface. Very often it pays to use a lightly weighted point fly in these circumstances so that you can keep the flies under the surface while retrieving quite quickly.

Another subtle method of achieving much the same effect is to use a sinking tip, which you can make yourself by splicing 5 yards of

AFTM 5 Wet Cel II on to an old no. 8 Longbelly or no. 9 Forward Taper. Do not buy sinking tips, nobody makes good ones commercially, but do not expect your homemade version to cast very pleasantly as it is fundamentally unbalanced in construction and will never perform really well.

Fish by casting out, letting the flies settle until you judge them to be at the right depth, and then retrieve at an appropriate speed. Takes tend to come in the first two or three pulls (often with vicious suddenness) or else as you lift off to recast. If the takes are coming early in the retrieve it often pays to stop after a dozen or so pulls and let everything settle a little before restarting. The right sort of flies to use for this are sedge pupae, small Jersey Herds, Invictas, Buff Buzzers and so on.

In flat calms it is sometimes possible to take the odd fish by throwing out three slow sinking flies and then waiting for a fish to rise somewhere near them. A couple of sharp pulls will either produce a truly vicious take or a complete lack of interest.

Topwater nymphing

As soon as you start to see fish rising, it is usually pointless to continue fishing deep. Heavy nymphs should be changed for light ones and, if it becomes obvious that fish are taking the fly in the surface film, either apply grease to your leader by dabbing it on with your fingers every foot or so, or use a point fly that will float if solidly greased such as a seal's fur buzzer or sedge; even buoyant nymphs have their place.

Terry Griffiths has devised a hatching buzzer dressing particularly appropriate for this situation in which he ties a bunch of pahmi fur projecting forwards over the eye of the hook, then 'parachutes' his hackle around the bunch of fur.

One has three basic options for catching topwater feeders:

(1) Cast out with greased line or fly and fish very slowly through the area of activity.
(2) Cast out with ungreased flies and fish them on a fast hand twist or pull retrieve to keep them up in the water.
(3) Using ungreased flies, cast upwind of risers and use pulling to induce the fish to take the fly.

Very frequently, you will be thoroughly baffled by your inability to interest rising fish – nothing is more frustrating. Often they are preoccupied with food forms that you aren't prepared for or just cannot imitate, the commonest of these being snails, pinfry, daphnia, microscopic buzzers and hatching buzzers.

Sometimes the only chance you may have of finding out what such fish are feeding on is to provoke one into having a go at something radically different – when desperate try Wake Muddlers, White Muddlers (just sub-surface), big White Lures or something Hot Orange.

One evening in May, 1974, I was fishing at anchor on the small side at Pitsford and I fished fruitlessly for 25 minutes during a very heavy rise. Eventually, I foul hooked a fish and an immediate insertion of the marrow scoop revealed large pale olive buzzers. Problem solved? Well, yes it was, but only because I knew of old that they would take bright apple green when hard on that particular buzzer. The result was 9 more fish for myself and Tony Knight before it was time to go. With preoccupied fish you either work the hatch or else knock them off their preoccupation with a joke fly.

Dry fly fishing

Late July, August and September are the best times to fish with the dry fly. I advise only half a dozen patterns: these include the Daddy long legs dressed in the Walker style with its legs trailing backwards, the Chestnut sedge, the sea-green bodied buffwinged sedge, the Sienna sedge, the Deer hair sedge and the Orgy fly in the evenings when clumps of mating sedges are about.

There isn't really a lot of technique involved in stillwater dry fly fishing. Grease your fly and use a leader 12 to 15 feet long, greased at intervals along its length.

This is one time when it can be profitable to fish a leeward shore anchored square-on; one merely casts out and watches for rises. It pays to fish fairly close to the boat, and when risers come upwind you can lift off and cover them quickly.

I make no claim of expertise at dry fly fishing in this style. Some years ago at Eyebrook I had the misfortune to take 6 fish in a day with the Daddy long legs; the misfortune was that 67 other fish had a go at the fly and I missed all of them.

Lures

I normally use only three lures when fishing anchored square-on and always as point flies. The Missionary, tied with the wing made from a spoon-shaped Silver Mallard pin feather (you get about 10 from a drake shot in October) laid flat over the back. This fly settles very very slowly and is used when you know that there are fry feeders about. The leaded Black Leech for fishing along the bottom in sink and draw style. Lastly, the double-ended Muddler is well worth fishing as a single heavily greased dry fly on evenings when the sedges are skittering along the top. This fly can be worked to make a considerable wake by being jerked, twitched or figure-of-eighted. Often the initial response is a splash as the fish tries to drown it and one then has to wait for the fish to come a second time and take a firm hold of the fly. That wait is very trying.

Obviously, square-on anchoring offers a wide scope for the individual to exercise his creativity. However, one final point of warning: even using the range of tactics outlined plus those of your own, you will probably find that a spot goes very cold after a while, and when this happens you have no option but to move. On a typical long summer's day at anchor, I suspect that you should move about every two hours. Usually all you need do is to row quietly 50 yards along the bank and then gently drop the anchors again and start afresh.

Nose-down anchoring

Nose-down anchoring as a technique has much more flexibility. I tend to associate it with fishing the lure; however, it can be used for almost all of the techniques outlined previously, the major exception being deep nymph fishing with the floating line.

Setting a boat to fish in nose-down style is accomplished by the following means: approach the desired spot from upwind and drop the anchor over the stern of the boat, tie the anchor to the stern or side quarter using a G-cramp to fine tune the setting and pay out line until you are where you want to be.

Boat organisation

There are basically two attachment positions for the anchor rope, the differences are these:

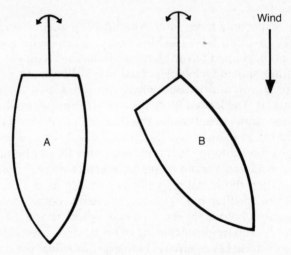

Fig. 6   Nose-down anchoring positions: (a) for light wind conditions,
(b) medium to heavy winds

Position A is only advised in light winds with a very competent caster sitting at the rear of the boat. This is because the man in the stern will always be casting with the wind coming over his wrong shoulder with the attendant problems of having flies stuck in the back of his head or blown into his face on the back cast.

In Position B the boat will tend to yaw about a little more; however, this is an easier position for the man in the stern to cast from.

If winds were always light, Position A would be the best option; alas, they aren't so one must use Position B and accept that the boat will swing about a bit. The boat should be organised as in Plate 4 with all surplus gear and rods out of the way and under cover. The net must always be to hand. When fishing each seat covers different water.

In terms of safety, there is only one real chance of accident and this is when the bow man casts into the overlap sector which can happen when a rising fish is seen approaching. Jim Clements and I have an understanding about this, when such a fish is spotted the

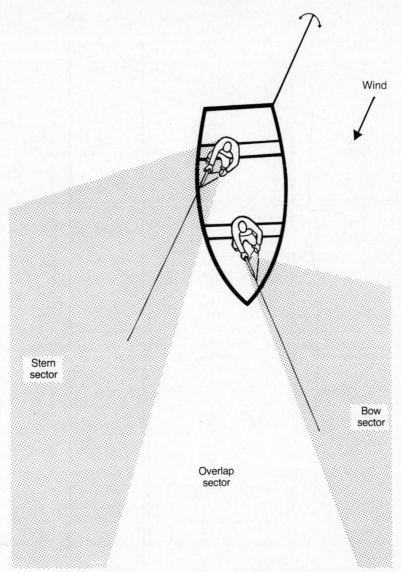

Wind

Stern
sector

Bow
sector

Overlap
sector

Fig. 7   Water coverage: nose-down anchoring

bow man shouts 'heads' and the stern man ducks until the cast is made.

The one major drawback of this style is that it will not work with partners who are not both right or both left handed.

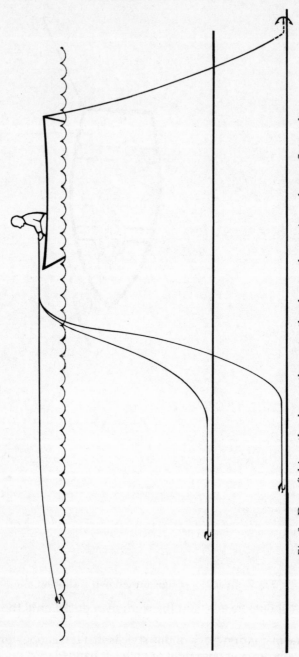

Fig. 8 Deep fishing: the deeper the water the shorter the retrieve along a flat track

Deep fishing

It is axiomatic that in order to fish deep from anchor and to cover a fair amount of ground with each retrieve, one needs to cast a very long way. From Fig. 8 you will see that the deeper you fish, the less bottom the retrieve covers before the fly starts to rise up towards the boat.

This distance can be increased by paying out line after you have cast, enabling the fly to fall without being pulled back towards the boat as the line tightens. Unfortunately, if you do pay out line, you will be unable to detect takes on the drop; in fact, you will probably never realise that such a take has occurred until you are woken from your reverie by the sight of a fish repeatedly leaping out of the water trying to rid itself of your fly.

The deeper you fish, the harder it is to present the fly effectively. In practice, it is rarely worth attempting to fish more than 40 feet deep although on certain reservoirs, notably Datchet, Foremark and Ladybower, it is occasionally profitable to fish about 70 feet down with the fly coming almost vertically upwards for most of the retrieve.

In order to fish depths of between 18 and 70 feet in this style only two lines are necessary: a Super Aquasinker shooting head and a Gladding Mark V 45 lb. test 30-foot leadcored shooting head (although the more adventurous may add the 450 grain Cortland Kerboom lead for massive distance casting and a formidable sinking speed).

Deep fishing demands the use of shooting heads, continuous lines are completely inadequate. The long casting requirement implies the use of heavy tackle.

Additionally, the wind plays a significant part in the choice. Sooner or later you will get caught in a wind in excess of force 5 Beaufort and when that happens you won't be able to backcast into it with line lighter than AFTM 10. There is only one case for using lighter line, and that is when fishing for surface feeders which will be disturbed by the splash of a heavy line hitting the water. If you are fishing deep, it doesn't hurt to put them down at all.

Leaders for shooting head work should not be complicated; I use 16 feet of level 13 lb. BS Racine Tortue as standard. On calm bright days, I might go down to 8 lb. BS Racine Tortue, never any lower. Frankly, you can fish with very heavy line on the big stillwaters, the only reservation I have is that you should match the shade of your monofil to the general colour of the water. Grafham and Rutland are normally greenish, Foremark is sandy brown at times. Pick your monofil to suit the water you fish.

Tactics

Depending upon the bottom conditions, you have two basic tactical options: if the bottom is weeded, the fly should be fished just above the weed; given a clean bottom, the fly can be fished along it. The first move at anchor over deep water is to establish whether you have clean bottom in any castable direction from the boat. If you have, then spend some time fishing with the fly coming hard along it.

Most of the time, the bottom will be weeded and it is very rare in my experience for a trout to take hold of a weeded fly; oddly enough, perch and pike will take a weeded fly almost as well as a clean one, but I can only once remember a trout doing so over the last ten years.

The trick in fishing deep over a weeded bottom, without spending most of the day removing debris from the hook, is to time the fall of the fly. I use a stopwatch; other people sit in their boats actually counting aloud to themselves, and this, if you try it for any length of time becomes very wearing indeed. The stopwatch has another major use and that is in dealing with a suspended population of fish feeding at a specific distance above the bottom. It is likely that you will encounter rainbows feeding in this manner sometime in the day, so when you anchor you must experiment to cover all depths, trying a series of 5, 10, 15 and 20 second drops, and so on. Working systematically with the stopwatch will give you the capability of fishing very accurately at a specific depth and, in addition, will tell you how deep the fish actually are feeding.

When fishing deep, takes tend to occur at three distinct moments in the retrieve:

(1)   Within the first few pulls.
(2)   As the fly lifts up off the bottom.
(3)   On the lift up into the surface.

One sometimes encounters problems with fish that tap at the fly or others that take hold on the pause between pulls.

The first two types of take are relatively easy, you miss them or you hook them and there isn't really any way that you can influence the outcome except to sharpen your hooks (see appendix IV) and to be poised to strike at all times.

Takes coming in the surface require a special approach. As you near the end of the retrieve hold the line in your retrieving hand and raise your rod sharply. When the rod has reached 11 o'clock stop and if your judgement of the amount of line outside the tip ring is correct then the fly will come to a halt just under the surface. If a fish is following the fly, the sudden spurt and halt given to the fly by this method (which I shall call 'the draw') will induce a take. Striking this type of take is not easy, you watch the fly coming up to the surface and strike when it disappears. You do this by lifting your rod hand further back (like a high backhand clear at badminton) while pulling down hard with the retrieving hand. This system of fishing out the last few pulls should be practised until it becomes automatic, as it applies not only to anchor fishing, but to all forms of lure fishing and some forms of wet fly fishing as well. Mastery of this technique will give you five fish where you had four before.

Tap takes are a problem. Far too many people make the mistake of striking hard at the slightest touch, but this is absolutely the wrong thing to do. There are several ways of dealing with tapping fish; the first is to maintain your retrieve at the same pace and get poised to strike if the fish comes again. The second method requires iron nerves: as soon as you feel a tap, stop stone dead and let the fly settle back for a second, then restart your retrieve but expect the fish to have taken the fly as it was falling back. Depending on the day, one method will work better than another. There are other tricks you may try in this situation, a favourite of mine is to speed the retrieve up until the end of the shooting head hits the tip ring, then stop everything and expect a take. Very occasionally an unevenly paced retrieve may pay dividends, all days and all situations vary and there is no certain rule in these matters.

Takes between the pulls are best detected by watching the curve the line makes between rod point and surface. As you pull the curve lifts up and as you go to regrip for another pull, the line settles back into the water; if it doesn't settle back, strike immediately. A major help is to use yellow fluorescent monofil, any slight delay shows up like a sore thumb.

Deep fishing flies

It is difficult to lay down any kind of law about the right flies to use for deep fishing as waters and conditions differ markedly; moreover, fish show preferences for lures on what appears to be a fairly random basis. However, one can say that in deep fishing, large flies are rather better than small ones, and the basic colours to concentrate on are blacks and whites. Orange, yellow and red flies are not usually very effective when used deeper than 20 feet. The most useful sizes tend to be 6 to 8 tandems and large single hooked flies from LS 4 to LS 6.

It is a good idea to carry a number of variations, and the likely flies in my boxes are:

Black Christmas Tree (tandem)	White tandem Marabou
Black Marabou (tandem)	White Matuka
Zuluka	Badger Matuka
Christmas Tree Matuka	White Lure with orange throat
Black Chenille Lure	Dog Nobblers
Black and Gold Hairwing	Zero
Bloody Maria Hairwing	Appetizer
White Christmas Tree (tandem)	Baby Doll

In practice, what you and your partner have to do is to conduct a series of complementary experiments until you find out which fly is working, at what depth and at what basic retrieve speed.

It is quite a fair tactic to go and anchor near another boat seen to be taking fish and watch what is happening; careful use of the stop-watch and an educated guess at what the successful fisherman has on the end of his leader should put you in touch with fish fairly quickly. However, the following points have a bearing on the advisability of staying.

Eyebrookitis

Years ago, at Eyebrook, I noticed a peculiar phenomenon which I now refer to as Eyebrookitis. The symptom is a large concentration of boats all fishing very closely together at anchor. When part of such a pack, it is as well to estimate the rate at which fish are being taken. For instance, with ten boats fishing, and one fish being taken every half hour, the catch rate is one fish per ten rod hours (two fishermen in a boat). If the rate is unsatisfactory, do not stay near such a pack of anchored boats.

Bottom features

Bottom features are very important in deep fishing, they tend to concentrate the fish around them in tight shoals. Should one or two boats be over such a favourable bottom, they will take fish, whereas other boats in close proximity will not.

One of the keys to successfully fishing deep is a detailed knowledge of the bottom contours of the reservoir. As outlined previously, the echo sounder and maps will tell you fairly rapidly where the interesting bottom features are; these are the places on which to focus your deep fishing: deeps around shoal water, old stream beds, submerged ditches, fences and roadways and, for those with large numbers of flies to lose, submerged timber.

I first began to use the echo sounder years ago at Draycote to find the edges of the shoals. It is very easy, one rows upwind towards a shoal, watches the echo sounder as the depth lifts from 50 to 20 feet, rows on a bit further, drops the anchor and fishes up the shoal bank. Over such a depth variation, you are almost bound to catch fish. Rutland and Grafham both contain several similar marks, as indeed do most other stillwaters.

Fishing medium-depth and shallow water

I regard different sinking lines much as a golfer regards his clubs: each line offers a range of options. If, for example, you wish to fish over 12 feet of water it is possible to do so in a variety of ways: with a leadcore shooting head you have to retrieve very quickly to prevent the fly from dragging in the weed; a Super Aquasinker allows you to fish at a slower pace over the same depth and a Wet Cel II at an easier pace yet. In other words you match the line to desired depth and retrieve speed. On the day the fish may want the fly coming fast or slow – you must satisfy them, not yourself.

In principle, fishing in medium to shallow depths of water is no different to fishing in the deeps. However more attention should be given to fishing the drop, the size of the flies should be reduced and the variety of patterns considerably widened.

When one sets out to take fish on the drop, certain modifications have to be made to one's approach. Long casting, for instance, ceases to be of critical importance, it is better to put the fly out 25 yards very quietly and carefully, ensuring that the leader turns over fully. Quietness is even more essential over shallow water. To increase one's chance of taking fish on the drop, slower sinking lines should be used than would be appropriate for fishing along the bottom. The longer it takes the fly to fall, the better. This method can be greatly assisted by using appropriately tied flies, the classic for this being the flat-winged Missionary. Specialists have been known to use a team of three variously sized Missionaries on a sink-tip shooting head to achieve an almost non-existent rate of fall.

It is essential that very close contact with the fly is maintained, and this is done by tightening up the line immediately after the cast has been made. If the boat yaws about, line must alternately be paid out and taken in to keep the contact close.

The best flies for fishing the drop are small white lures like the Missionary, Appetizer or Baby Doll. Using these flies tends to work best on rainbows in water which contains a fair concentration of fry. One critical feature of the construction of a lure for drop fishing is that it must be a single action fly, it must work in the water as a unified entity without the hinging, for instance, that comes from using a marabou wing. It is, additionally, advantageous if the wing does not twist under the hook bend for this affects the action of the fly and causes it to twist on the retrieve. Trout stay away from twisting flies, as a rule.

Mid-depth fishing produces a large number of induced takes in the early part of the retrieve cycle. Fish will watch a fly fall and then attack it as soon as it is pulled away from them, so beware of line burns from the monofil. These can be avoided by the simple expedient of filling your coffee cup with water and dipping your index finger into it before starting the retrieve.

Judgement of depth over weed is more critical in shallow water than in deep. My best day of rainbow fishing, at Rutland in 1980 (four for 15 lb. 3 oz. in six hours' fishing) was in 8 feet of water, all the fish coming to a size 8 long shank Zuluka and all taken on a Garcia slow sinker taking one minute and six seconds to drop – four seconds more put the fly into the weed every time!

Several experts I know are fishing with compound shooting heads made of lengths of level Aquasink, Wet Cel and Floater so as to bounce the line belly on the bottom whilst the fly rides above it. Together with semi-buoyant lures, this is another solution to the problem of fishing just above weed.

Small flies

It is comparatively easy to fish deep with a team of nymphs, pupae or traditional wet flies on a sinking or sink-tip shooting head. I usually reserve this tactic for those days on which trout steadfastly refuse to have anything to do with a fly larger than a size 12. Ultimately, the only thing you cannot do effectively with a shooting head and a team of three is to figure-of-eight retrieve; sink and draw fishing, however, is simple.

Not only is it possible to fish at depth with insect imitations; one can also, by judicious use of an odd split shot (if the rules permit it) generate an exaggerated sink and draw retrieve that will, on occasion, prove highly effective.

Competitive urges

At certain times of the year, in waters containing rainbows, it is possible to exploit the competitive urge of these fish. One achieves this by rigging the dropper within 2 feet of the point fly using a large lure on the point and a small lure, or even a pupa, on the dropper. Often it pays to use a brightly coloured dropper, particularly a hot-orange one. Rainbows are aggressive fish, happy to compete with one another in a shoal, darting in to snatch food from in front of the mouths of their fellows. A large lure chasing a small one can trigger off just this reaction. And if you get the fish really annoyed, it may even bite at the competition, the large lure on the point. Normally, though, fish will hit the dropper, often very hard indeed!

Wind, currents and clouded water

If one spends a whole day at anchor one will encounter patchy feeding at different times of the day. Fish will come on and go off the feed as if a switch was turned, and it is difficult to know if the reluctance of the fish to take the fly is due to fear or plain disinterest. Having taken a better fish or two it is often hard to decide whether to move and try elsewhere or to wait it out until they resume feeding. In these situations, I frequently feel that I get it wrong more often than not.

An easier choice to make is whether or not to fish on the upwind or the lee shore. Winds of force 2–4 Beaufort usually make for better anchor fishing conditions than very heavy winds, as the option of fishing the downwind shore remains feasible.

Stillwaters are never stillwaters when there is wind. By careful observation of your home water in heavy wind conditions you will notice stain lines and other indications of current movements developing. The most important of these are the currents that develop along a shore for these tend to attract the fish into them. There are also the currents which underlie the waves, flowing against the main direction of the wind. Stain lines and currents concentrate fish.

When you come to fish in a current, it is best to fish on the swing with a medium sinking or sink-tip line. One casts across the direction of the current and then waits to allow the current to swing the fly round until the line straightens out downstream before beginning the retrieve.

Stained water invariably attracts rainbows. The standard tactics are to anchor close to the stain to cast just into it and then retrieve your fly out and into clear water where hungry fish are waiting. Often though I have found that the fish are in a denser concentration thirty yards upwind from a stain than they are in it, and this is a point worth remembering. Stains tend to move out from the bank during the course of the day, and it is important to keep an eye on this and to move with it.

Nose upwind anchoring

In a particularly severe wind when a boat cannot be held at stern anchor, it may hold anchored by the bow. Boats so anchored yaw considerably, to such an extent as to render fishing almost impossible. It is a tactic of last resort and not to be generally recommended.

══ 3 ══ *Over the front* ══

Most drift fishing is over the front fishing in one form or another. It is a particularly deadly method when conditions are appropriate and a hopeless waste of time when conditions are not. Two friends fished over the front at Rutland for the first ten days of the opening season and took only 14 fish between them; somewhat later in the year they went out for the day and were forced off the water at 1.15 p.m. having taken 32 fish since 9 a.m.

For successful fishing over the front the fish must be feeding high in the water, certainly no deeper than 4 feet and, preferably, within a foot of the surface. This requirement means that it is most effective between late May and late September. The proclivity of stillwater trout to come up to the surface only early and late in the day further limits the effectiveness of over the front techniques. Yet this style is probably the most appropriate one on three days out of ten throughout the season. Certainly nobody can be an adequate boat fisherman without having a thorough grasp of its principles and applications.

Boat control

Boat control is the first feature of forward fishing to be mastered. In earlier, more leisured times, this skill barely concerned the fisherman who would have employed the services of a boatman or ghillie; even today, mainly in Ireland and Scotland it is still possible to engage a ghillie to whom one can leave the whole problem of boat control. Yet on most of the waters that I fish regularly, it is an offence to employ someone to manoeuvre the boat with the oars whilst fishing is taking place.

The main duty of the boatman, apart from the obvious and laborious one of rowing a pair of paying customers back upwind, was to hold the boat steady on the drift. While in England at least, the boatman may have gone, the problem remains. I cannot recall fishing from a boat that has drifted, on its own accord, smoothly and steadily downwind. Uneven weight loading in the boat or a screwed keel make a boat drift off line. If you are having problems with a boat, experiment with the positions of the heavier elements of your equipment. A judicious movement of gear, perhaps assisted by swapping ends with your partner if he is heavier or lighter than you, can often see the problems disappear.

Why should a boat be set up to drift in a dead straight line down-wind? If the boat doesn't drift straight then one partner will find that his companion is catching all the fish while he is having a hard time just casting. Even a slight crosswind drift can make one partner's life very hard; an acute crosswind drift may confound his fishing day altogether.

The drogue

A more certain way of countering crosswind drifts is to use drogues. Drogues in the plural, as the use of a single drogue tends to make the boat yaw, and the longer the rope the drogue is on the more pronounced the yaw will be, just as in side-on anchor fishing. Drogues have the principal function of slowing down the rate of a boat's advance. It is possible to drift at such a speed that even the fastest retrieve will not keep one from over-running the flies. Winds in excess of Beaufort 4 necessitate the use of drogues.

I carry three drogues. The two main ones are 4 feet square with a 4-inch diameter hole in the centre. The corner cords are light terylene 2 feet 6 inches long and tied to the end of a small swivel. The fixing rope linking the boat to the other end of the swivel is 6 feet of polypropylene washing line. The third drogue is very much smaller (one foot square braking area) and of the windsock design, which is useful as it sets itself in the water without one having to pull at it to get it to unfurl. Braking and balancing is achieved by setting the two large drogues out of the back and at opposite ends of the boat, attaching them to the top of the thwarts with good solid 6-inch G-cramps. The smaller drogue is only brought into play for fine balancing the boat, on its own in a light wind, or added to the two larger drogues.

It is essential to carry one's own drogues as most drogues supplied by water authorities tend to be either too small, incorrectly designed or affixed a long way from the point of balance of the boat. For those unable or unwilling to manufacture their own drogues, Bob Church supplies very adequate ones; the Saville patented easy-retrieve drogue is also recommended.

It is possible to set up a boat with a large rudder for perfect control of side-on drifting. This can be done in one of two ways (see Fig. 9). Using the rudder one has no need to bother with arranging the boat's weight loading or with paying special attention to the positioning of the drogues (those interested in constructing such rudders should refer to the appendix).

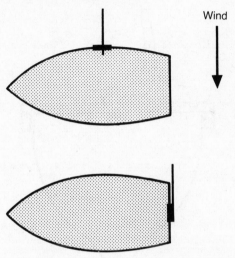

Wind

Fig. 9 Rudder control of side on drifting; either attachment position works

Once you have gained control of the drifting boat, the next concern is the organisation of the boat. Use should be made of plankseats to go across the thwarts; it is better to sit level with the thwarts than to attempt to fish over the top of them as it were. For sufferers of back and bottom ache, the design for a fighting chair (Fig. 10) will prove beneficial (see appendix VII for elaboration).

Before moving on to actual fishing, a point about safety must be made. The same hazard of hooking one's partner applies here as in square-on anchor fishing. As more rising fish are covered when drifting, the chance of inadvertently hooking your partner is increased.

Both partners should wear some form of eye and head protection, prescription spectacles and baseball caps have served me well enough for a decade and have prevented a considerable number of mishaps in that time. I always put the hood of my coat up whenever the wind starts to blow, apart from the safety consideration it protects the back of my head and neck from the wind.

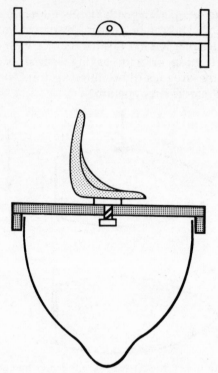

Fig. 10   Swivel fighting chair

Shortlining

The traditional style of over the front fishing is known as shortlining or loch style fishing. As the name, shortlining, suggests, one does not cast far from the boat, in fact the technique has been referred to as augmented dapping. The technique requires a long light rod as it relies heavily on very accurate control of the movement of the bob fly and this is only truly possible when using rods of 10 feet in length or more.

The practice is to cast a short line no longer than twice the length of the rod and to fish by a combination of raising the rod (so that the flies glide back towards the fisherman) and retrieving. There are several small but important variations that can affect the action of the flies.

(1) Holding on to the line with the retrieving hand and raising the rod in a controlled fashion with the other. Depending on the speed of the raise the flies will either remain stationary in the water or will move smoothly towards the boat. The line *must* be sufficiently heavy not to be bellied outwards by the wind.

(2) Figure-of-eight retrieving while simultaneously raising the tip of the rod. This produces a rather faster fly action.

(3) Varying the rod lift to produce a miniature spurt-pause retrieve.

Fish often show a distinct preference for one variation or the other depending on the day, so ringing the changes is essential.

The construction of the leader is critical, particularly in obtaining close control over the action of the flies. The distance between the top dropper and the end of the flyline must be varied according to the strength of the wind from between four and eight feet. The stronger the wind, the further the dropper should be from the end of the flyline. Similarly, the length of the top dropper itself should be varied from three to six inches depending on the height of the waves; the higher the wave the longer the dropper. Indeed, the whole of the leader must be adjusted to suit the wind strength so that each fly can be made to work attractively as it reaches the surface. The distance between the flies should also be adjusted to suit the wind strength, from between 3 and 6 feet apart. Exploring these subtle variations can make the difference between a limit and a blank, as can exploring the combinations of weighted and un-weighted flies.

The flyline must be as light as possible. It should be a double taper, because frequently the top dropper will be fished within a few feet of the tip of the line and fish that rise immediately in front of the boat have to be covered at very close range. A heavy delivery will inevitably result in spooked fish.

For a rod, I recommend either one of the 11-foot carbon rods purpose-built by Bob Church, or one self-assembled from the excellent 12-foot Fibatube carbon blanks. The serious shortline fisherman requires two rods, one to match a DT 5 and one to match a DT 7 to cope with greater wind speeds.

Casting and retrieving a short line must be practised until the actions are simple and automatic. The angler's attention must be focussed exclusively on the water immediately behind the flies in anticipation of a sub-surface taker or a fish coming to the bob fly, particularly at the very end of the retrieve. Roll-over rises may confuse the beginner as an immediate strike usually yields nothing. When a roll-over occurs count 'one' and strike on 'two'. Long, light rods do not put heavy pressure on fish and it is safe to fish with a lighter leader – I recommend 5 lb. BS Tynex.

Shortlining is not a technique for calm, bright days as the fish have to be close in to the boat. Certainly a ripple helps conceal angler and boat from the fish. In Ireland and Scotland where the technique originated on low-pressure fisheries, it is common for fish to come close in to the boat to take the fly. At places like Rutland and Grafham, however, there are about 20 boats fishing per 1,000 acres on every day of the season. By the autumn, the fish have definitely become wary of the boats, and the effectiveness of shortlining diminishes.

Shortlining is probably the best way of representing a hatch of fly, as it is possible, on a three-fly cast, to present a pupa, a hatching pupa and a dry fly coming off at the same time. Dealing, for instance, with a hatch of red chironomids, a typical set-up would be a red buzzer on the point, a Woodcock and red on the dropper and a Soldier Palmer on the bob.

When rising fish cease to come close enough to the boat to be caught by shortlining, a change of approach is called for. It is time to tackle up for long range fishing in front of the boat, probably the most popular style of over the front fishing in England.

Longlining

Firstly, the boat should be slowed down to a pace which allows the flies to be fished with a pull retrieve of a foot or so without contact being lost or the boat overrunning the line. Big drogues are essential for this.

I use the same tackle as for bankside nymphing. A 10-foot AFTM 6/7 Lamiglas Blank casting DT 5 and 6 lines (the 6 for the windy days), 100 yards of 20 lb. BS monofil backing held on a Fishhawk or Speedex multiplier reel. With this tackle, I can cast about 28 yards of line fairly easily.

I use double tapered lines exclusively for this form of fishing; not so much because they are easy to cast a long way but because one can lift the flies off the water a long way out, change direction on the back cast and drop the flies in front of a rising fish.

Better lines for long distance casting, the forward taper and long-belly, have to be retrieved until the belly is within a yard of the rod tip before one can lift them off and throw at a fish. Often the extra time this takes means that the chance has gone.

I advise beginners to use the 10-foot 6/7 Lamiglas but with a forward tapered 7 or longbelly 6. When casting skills improve, then move to using a double taper.

When I began boatfishing, I came under the influence of Arthur Cove and the late Ken Jacobs. As a result when longlining I always ensure that there is a lot of nylon between the end of the fixed loop and the point fly. I rarely longline three flies forward with less than 18 feet of leader; in tricky, still conditions I have fished with up to 24 feet of leader, more than that I cannot handle comfortably. It is only sensible to present the flies as far away as possible from the disturbance caused by the flyline.

Leaders should be constructed on the Cove principle laid out in the chapter on anchor fishing (see page 16). Remember that the longer the leader the greater the need for a heavy point fly. I nearly always load the point with a size 8 heavy wire Cove's Pheasant Tail (tied on a Mustad 7780c) – it is one of the great flies for fishing over the front.

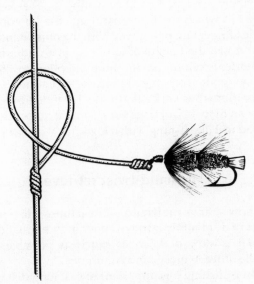

Fig. 11 The necking loop

Leader material is of some importance here. I have tried many leader materials and have settled on 5 lb. and 6 lb. BS Tynex in continuous lengths. I make my own leaders from level monofil using either a 4-turn Cove Knot or a 5-turn Blood Knot to form the droppers. Tynex has considerable resistance to sudden takes and about the only way in which it can be broken is when a necking loop has formed in casting. The necking loop reduces the breaking strain of any monofil by about 70 per cent. One must examine the leader every so often to ensure that one has not formed. You can be certain that if a fish makes off with all your flies then it undoubtedly did so by taking the top dropper with one of these nasty little knots in it. Wind knots also reduce leader strength, though they aren't nearly as dangerous as the necking loop.

One means of fishing with fine monofil down to 3 lb. BS without being repeatedly broken is to tie 6 inches of Optima Power Gum between the monofil and the tip of the flyline. Power Gum deteriorates quite rapidly and must be replaced at least fortnightly or immediately, after a hard fight with a large fish.

The pull retrieve

The most widely used method of activating the flies is through the pull retrieve, in which the fisherman traps the line under the rod holding index finger and pulls away with the other hand. I point the rod straight down the line holding the tip just under or above the surface. I retrieve 'blind', paying little attention to the fly except when it is being lifted up prior to recasting. Because I feel for the takes, carbon fibre rods are better for the job than fibreglass or cane ones. The sensitivity of carbon is surprising, it makes fishing with a fibreglass rod feel like fishing with a log.

The hand-twist retrieve

Trout can show strange preferences and at times will refuse a pulled fly in favour of a smoothly retrieved one. In this situation, it is vital that the boat is slowed down as much as possible. Two large drogues will suffice in most wind conditions.

In hand-twist fishing it is important to cast long distances (25–30 yards) and to use long leaders from 15 to 24 feet. It is not a good idea to stand up whilst casting, particularly in calm conditions, as this puts the fish down at very much greater distances than is commonly realised.

A good tip is to cast out and allow up to fifteen seconds to lapse before starting to move the flies. During this time the line should be retrieved at the speed of the boat's advance. Very often, a fish will either take the fly (particularly the point fly) as it falls, or track the fly and then take it as the retrieve is started.

Always vary the action, pace and, in pull retrieving, the length of pull. Further variations can be produced by using leaded flies or by pinching split shot on to the leader (when the rules allow). For the opposite effect, grease is useful. The way in which I do this is to grease the flyline tip solidly, and the leader in patches, down to the top dropper, one or two dabs of grease between the top and middle droppers and no grease whatsoever between the point fly and middle dropper. This arrangement will put the bob fly on top of the surface film, the second fly in it and the point fly just submerged. Depending on the size and style of the dressings, it may be necessary to grease the flies as well.

When using grease, one must be very aware of changing conditions: as the wind dies away in the evening the grease becomes more effective than in daytime wave conditions. It may then become necessary to adjust the greasing to ensure that the flies are working properly – always carry a degreaser.

Rising fish

There are several ways of dealing with rising fish, but one rule applies to them all: the flies must be delivered well ahead of the fish. It is extremely rare in my experience for a fish to turn round and have a go.

This usually means casting upwind of the rise, the exception being when fishing down slick lanes when it is not uncommon for fish to be travelling downwind. How does one cover such a fish without lining him? The answer is in a very precise delivery and braking of the shoot, so that only the leader and the flies enter the trout's vision.

Ordinarily, the best practice is to drop the flies three to four feet upwind of a riser, pause to let them fall through the surface film and then to begin a steady pull when the fish is judged to be a foot or so away from them.

Normally it pays to fish at a slight sideways angle and to retrieve the flies outside the drift path of the boat. Fish tend to run straight up the wind; in quiet wind and on odd pale grey-light days they can undoubtedly spot a boat at up to 20 yards. Fish moving just wide of the boat usually come much closer before taking fright.

Occasionally fish will move upwind at an angle, making one seat in the boat more profitable than the other. The only way of sharing the fishing in this situation is to change seats with your partner!

Sometimes a fish will rise on a line closer to the boat than the flies in the water. When this happens, retrieve the flies quickly and then stop the retrieve when the flies are directly upwind of where you anticipate the fish to be. Restart the retrieve as soon as you estimate that the fish has reached the flies.

Sub-surface feeding

When fish are rising there is no point in fishing with anything other than a floater. However, when they are feeding on submerged insects you should use a sink-tip line. The one I use is made by splicing five yards of tapered AFTM 5 Wet Cel II to the end of a WF 7 longbelly. I only use this line when the hand-twist retrieve is called for.

When fishing the sink and draw method, however, I use a sink-tip shooting head. It has much to commend it in terms of distance and lack of effort, though one must always be careful to cast a wide open loop in both backcast and forecast, otherwise quite remarkable tangles occur.

By using the sinking tip and delaying the start of the retrieve it is possible to fish a range of depths.

Sub-surface feeding can take place on very rough days. On such occasions it is worth remembering two things in particular: firstly, use a slow sinking line (often a sink-tip will not penetrate surface turbulence quickly enough) and secondly, remember that the boat will calm the water for a considerable distance downwind. This calmer water is in a V-shape and it often pays to cast into the tip of the vee.

Fishing deep

When fishing on a water that does not allow Northampton style, one has to accommodate for fish feeding at greater depths than can be effectively covered by conventional means. Friends of mine have been known to use heavy forward tapered lines, like Wet Cel II and Super Aquasinker, casting as far as possible, letting the flies sink and then pulling like madmen to produce a deep retrieve before the line goes underneath the boat.

By using a leadcore shooting head, with the boat drogued heavily it is possible to fish forwards and get the fly down as deep as 20 feet. However the retrieve track is erratic, the casting is dangerous and the tactic generally unproductive.

When fish are feeding deep one must get the flies down to them or face the prospect of going home fishless. If over the front tactics are the only ones allowed on your local water my advice is to fish at anchor. It is by far the most efficient way of reaching the right depth.

Surface lure fishing

Very frequently, fish running close to the surface can be taken on lures. Some trout find the fast movement of a lure irresistible and the general rule for this type of surface fishing is to retrieve as fast as possible.

Oddly, fish running high in the water will sometimes refuse to chase a lure presented straight down the wind. Generally it is better to retrieve upwind and across.

Surface lure fishing is really a target game, the object being to drop the lure just beyond and wide of a fish and to then induce a take. A properly presented lure should be pulled past the fish's nose and then away rapidly. Drop the fly just wide of the fish as illustrated (Fig. 12) and judge the first pull to bring the fly into the trout's vision. The take can be expected within the next two or three pulls.

Occasionally, a fish will chase after the fly making a visible wake: there are two ways of hooking these fish. In my view, the most effective is to retrieve flat out and prepare for a relatively gentle take. The alternative method is to stop and restart the retrieve and to expect the fish to take hold of the fly on the pause. When a fish breaks the water on the fly, count two and strike hard!

The final draw is an important part of this technique as a fish will often chase the fly right up until it stops on the surface and then take hold of it. A useful tip is to swing the fly slightly sideways at the end

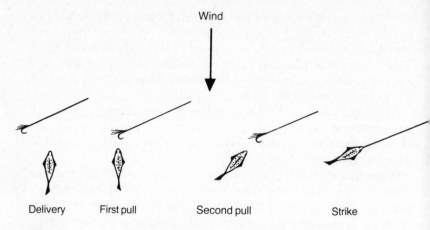

Fig. 12 Sideways induction by overshoot casting and timing the first
pull to bring the fly past the fish's nose

of the retrieve so that the fish is not presented with a head-on view
of boat and fisherman just as it is about to take the fly.

The rods and lines for this are those for light shooting heads. I use
a 10 ft. 6 in. Fibatube Carbon blank matched to a 33-foot AFTM 9
shooting head.

Depth is critical and there are three ways in which a lure can be
surface fished; on the day one will usually prove more attractive to
the fish than the others.

(1) In the surface film, fished to produce wake. For real effective-
     ness use a semi-buoyant lure like a heavily-dressed well-
     greased Muddler (the Ogston, Keetley and double-ended
     variations are all appropriate). I have tried popping or
     chugging bass bugs and given them up. Muddlers are more
     effective and do not make that rather embarrassing 'poc, poc,
     poc' noise.
(2) The retrieve in which the lure runs immediately below the
     surface film and creates a wake without actually breaking the
     surface.
(3) The wake-free retrieve with an ordinary lure or tube fly. At
     high speed it is almost mandatory to fish the lure on a sink-tip
     to prevent it lifting in the water and producing a wake. The best
     flies for this through the daytime are the Appetizer and the
     small White Tube, both lightweight and streamlined in profile.

For fry-feeding fish a very small Baby Doll or White Rabbit Nymph are killing patterns. Match lure size to fry size.

With surface lure fishing, there is the chance of provoking a fairly savage take, particularly from big fish. It is not a technique that requires fine tackle. As ever, I recommend heavy monofil – 13 lb. BS Racine Tortue and between 14 and 15 feet in length.

Muddler fishing

Muddler fishing is the best surface lure technique. It comes into its own as a successful daytime technique twice in the season. First, when daytime surface feeding begins during late May or early June. Secondly, about a week after the sedge hatch gets underway, usually during July.

White Muddlers, particularly the Keetley variation, start to produce well, from the appearance of pin fry onwards.

Evening Muddler fishing is spasmodically effective from opening day through to the end of September. It is usually better on warm nights when there is a little ripple and the odd slick lane about.

Two-fly induction has a place in surface muddler fishing, nowhere more than in the tactical variation known as the 'Acme Thunderer' developed by Nev Dickinson, his brother and Dave Greaves some years ago.

The Acme Thunderer rig consists of a large muddler on an L/S 6 or 4 with a pronounced squarely cut and well greased head as point fly, and an L/S 8 Squirrel and Orange on the dropper in front. This rig should be fished on a floating shooting head or a longbelly by casting as far as is humanly possible and then pulling as if demented. The muddler will alternately bounce over and then, due to the weight of the dropper, plunge under the surface resurfacing between pulls; all in all making a quite startling amount of commotion.

This method works best on grey days when there is a fair amount of ripple. Heavy leaders are essential because takes can be ferocious in the extreme, half coming to the Muddler and half to the Squirrel and Orange. On odd days, a Baby Doll or a small Black Lure with green fluorescent tail and cheeks works well on the dropper.

The name comes from Nev Dickinson's habit, announcing his success to those in the know by blowing on his accursed Acme Thunderer Whistle every time he caught another one.

Short takers

Surface lure stripping produces a considerable number of short takers. One way to hook short takers is to use a lure equipped with a flying treble hook. Terry Griffiths and Stewart Billam independently devised very similar solutions, they wire a small flying treble to the lure (see appendix). Flies dressed on Waddington Elverine mounts are highly efficient solutions to the same problem.

Deeper lure fishing

The best practice for deep fishing over the front with a lure has been developed by Terry Griffiths and Ian Grant. By using a large drogue off the stern quarter (see Fig. 13), the boat can be drifted slowly even in a heavy wind. Both partners cover different water and can present their flies in a different manner from one another if they so wish.

The boat moves sufficiently slowly for the stern man to allow his flies to fall much as if at anchor. The bow man has a better angle in terms of covering fish but a harder time casting across wind. Two other effective variations for this style of drifting are those involving muddler and buzzer combinations and the plunging fly.

One works the muddler and buzzer trick by rigging a small muddler (LS 8 or 10) as the greased point fly. White or standard muddlers or a flatwinged Missionary are the best for this. Two buzzer pupae are used as droppers and the leader can be fairly short, about 14 feet. It is fished by the bow partner only, who casts sideways from the line of drift and then either holds on to the line so that it swings slowly round or assists it by hand-twist retrieving.

The plunging fly technique involves the use of a leaded point fly dressed on a size 8 roundbend hook. With chenille body and a long marabou tail the fly is very reminiscent of a tadpole in shape. Terry Griffiths, whose fly this is, favours a black tail and a body of black and fluorescent green banded chenille.

One can pitch this fly onto the nose of a riser but it is normally cast out and allowed to fall and then worked back in sink and draw style.

Alternative boat manipulation

The leeboard has the ability to push the boat on a sharp crosswind

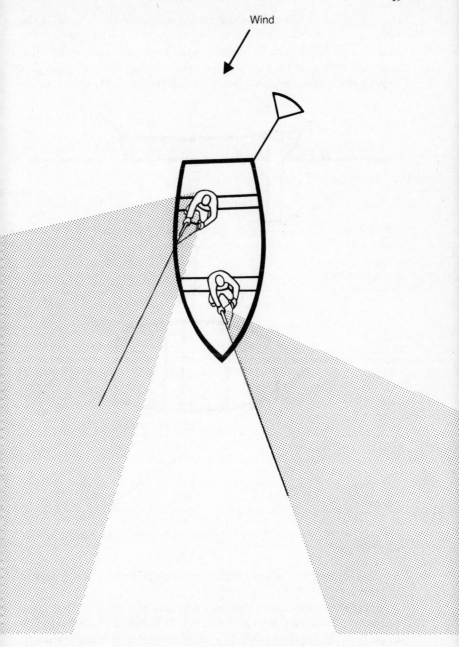

Wind

Fig. 13 Stern quarter drogue drifting

drift. Leeboards should be attached only to the bow curve of the boat, as a central fix will result in splintering the thwart. The stresses imposed on a leeboard by a heavy wind and wave are considerable and can damage the boat. A leeboard should not be used in a windspeed exceeding Beaufort 3. Attach the leeboard with a single

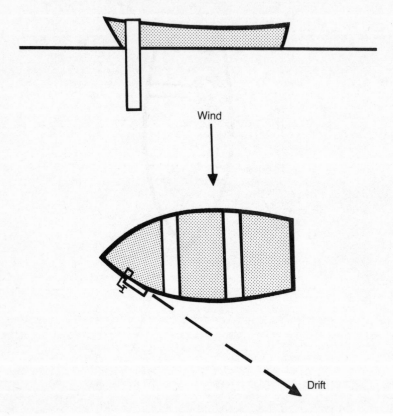

Fig. 14   Leeboard attachment and effect upon line of drift

6-inch G-cramp on the side nearest the bow, clamping it securely to the thwart.

Much the same effect can be obtained by using a very large (minimum area 4 sq. ft.) rudder attached to the stern and set at an angle (see Fig. 15). By casting at an angle of about 10° wide of straight downwind one can retrieve across the noses of the fish.

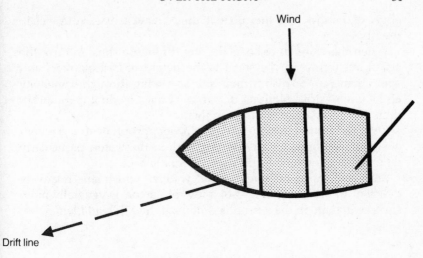

Fig. 15   Achieving the leeboard effect with a large rudder (4½ square feet)

Basic tactics

All drift fishing is a matter of finding the drifting line that fish are working on a particular day. Interestingly, a good top fishing line is rarely a good deep fishing line. Also it is unusual for the fish to be evenly distributed down a drift and it is always a good idea when one has drifted through a shoal of fish, to motor around and fish through the shoal again.

Except when there are slick lane formations or shallow shoaling water, it is generally better to concentrate your daytime drift fishing within a couple of hundred yards of the shore. One rarely encounters large numbers of fish over deep water during the day unless there has been a recent heavy stocking.

Slick lanes must be fished, almost invariably they contain fish but I prefer to drift along the side of the slick with one partner fishing slightly across the slick and the other fishing the rippled water beside it. The reason is that slick water is easy for fish to see in; they will be spooked a long way in front of the boat. By fishing the slick from the side, with the boat partially concealed by the ripple and with only the flies going into the slick, a greater number of fish will be taken.

In addition, fish often take very much better in the ripple near the edges of the slick than they do in it; they cannot see nearly as well in the ripple.

When there are other boats drifting through a shoal in turn, the act of anchoring on the shoal is the height of bad manners and sportsmanship. So also is motoring or rowing through somebody else's line of drift. Nothing disperses surface feeding fish quicker than a motorboat driven through them.

Over the front techniques are the most appropriate to use whenever the feeding trout are running high in the water, particularly when feeding on food forms capable of imitation.

Surface fishing on oligotrophic waters, which are relatively deficient in bottom feed and of a low ph factor, is generally more successful than on the eutrophic waters of the Midland Plain.

4   Dapping

Dapping is probably the original method our forebears used to fish the surface fly from boats; certainly, the old prints that I have seen suggest so. It still has a significant place in modern boatfishing at specific times of year and under particular conditions. It is also one of the most entertaining ways of fishing and can be most exciting when a fish comes up to inspect the fly before taking it. The tension at such a time can be almost unbearable, undoubtedly contributing to the many missed takes that occur while dapping.

For me, dapping starts in August and runs through to the end of September and it is principally associated with the Crane fly or Daddy long legs which makes its appearance during that period. In some years, if the winter has been severe, the Daddy does not show up at all, in other years it may emerge in considerable numbers.

A few years ago, I spent a considerable amount of time dapping throughout a season. It may have been a poor season for the surface fly but for much of the time my efforts did not yield many fish. It became clear that to entice fish it was necessary to use fairly small flies; most of the fish I took in the earlier half of the season were on size 10 Red Sedges. The main disadvantage of using small dapping flies is that they are hard to see on the water, especially when the wind is creating a wave. Later in the season, with larger flies hatching, one can increase the size of the artificial fly and the business of watching for takes is made easier.

Dapping is like kite flying really, the fly isn't the kite however, the line fulfils that function. To fly a kite the right amount of wind is crucial. Likewise, dapping becomes impossible in flat calms or very light airs and is equally difficult in heavy winds which blow the line about uncontrollably, the fly spending more time in the air than on the water. There are ways of coping with different wind speeds and these really rely on two factors, the length of the rod and the composition of the floss blowline.

I acquired a traditional heavy dapping rod about 13 years ago and still fish with it when the wind is not too strong. Made in the late 1890s by Gray's of Inverness, it is a 15-foot three-piece wholecane rod with the tip spliced midway into hexagonal split cane. Although it creaks and groans a bit, it has had a number of three-pound rainbows from Grafham and the odd four-pound brownie from Rutland. Alas, it weighs just over three pounds when fully assembled with a reel added. In a big wind I sometimes feel I am getting more sport out of playing the rod than the fish.

The ideal dapping rod is light and long, and for most of my dapping I use a 15-foot telescopic Shakespeare rod (serial number 1081-465, economy series). With a little modification to the positioning of the reel fitting it makes an excellent dapping pole. The rod could be even longer – 17½ to 20 feet – but less than 15 feet is not advisable except in very heavy wind conditions.

The type of dapping floss is critical to success. Over the years, I have acquired three different ones that enable me to cope with a wide range of wind conditions.

(1) A very light Shakespeare Fishhawk blowline of stranded crimplene.
(2) A medium-weight Spinnaker blowline made of stranded crimplene from Don's of Edmonton.
(3) An old heavy floss silk blowline.

One can make dapping lines from machine crimplene (incidentally, a very good substitute for silk tying thread in dressing large flies and lures). All one does is double, treble or quadruple the crimplene to make a line about 15 yards long, the strands secured by knotting it every foot or so.

I use a Speedex multiplier to hold the line and a hundred or so yards of scrap monofil shooting line as backing. Every fish has to be played off the reel so it is important to have one that works well. I always use multiplying fly reels when in a situation that requires fish to be played off the reel, largely because of the risk of a fish running straight towards the boat. The multiplier enables one to keep up with a fish and maintain a tight line throughout.

The nylon leader is almost unnecessary in dapping. In theory, it should be possible to present only the fly on the water, never the line. In practice after an hour or so, even a beginner will be able to present just the fly to the fish. One will still need a margin for error in the form of a leader of around 4 feet long. On windy days, one should even extend the leader as it has considerably less wind resistance than the blowline giving one greater control over the fly. Remember that with short leaders, the elasticity is reduced and there is an increased danger of being smashed on a hard take. The rule is to use stout line: 13 lb. BS Racine Tortue has always served me well.

Control of the boat is achieved in the same way as in over the front fishing. However, if the wind dies it becomes increasingly difficult to distance the fly from the boat (dapping works on windspeed relative to boat speed) and it is possible to create a higher relative windspeed by droguing the boat.

The key to effective dapping is to fish the fly on as short a line as is possible, while presenting the fly far enough away from the boat for the fish not to be spooked. As a rough guide the fly should be fished between 5 and 12 yards in front of the boat.

Fish can be persuaded to take the fly very much closer to the boat than 5 yards, but to achieve this stillness and camouflage are essential. Two things warn a trout of danger: movement and alien colours suddenly looming into their view. The common practice of the man on the left hand side of the boat dapping whilst his partner longlines a team of three will usually ensure that no dapping takes occur within 10 yards of the boat. The frequent movements of the caster guarantee visual disturbance.

Camouflage used by puntgunners is interesting in that it shows what has to be worn to approach an even warier prey than the trout. The traditional and well-proven garb of the puntgunner is an off-white smock and balaclava. A far cry from the dark olive oilskin jacket and oddly coloured headgear favoured by the fishermen I know.

The reason for fishing at close range becomes apparent when one considers exactly what happens when dapping. The wind, in blowing the fly away from the boat, causes a large belly in the line. Beyond about 15 yards this belly becomes truly enormous, making it virtually impossible to strike quickly. Here one has to rely on the chance of the fish making off with the fly and keeping on going until it has obligingly taken up most of the slack. Frankly, this seldom happens when using an artificial fly; a fish will spit it out far too quickly.

Dapping is actually so simple that it requires very few words to describe how to conduct it. Pull about 7 or 8 yards of blowline out of the tip ring (taking care not to drop it in the water), hold the rod well up and let it carefully blow out in front of the boat. Attempt to keep the fly on the surface at all times and move it from side to side by leading it with the rod tip. Gusts are the main bedevilment: as soon

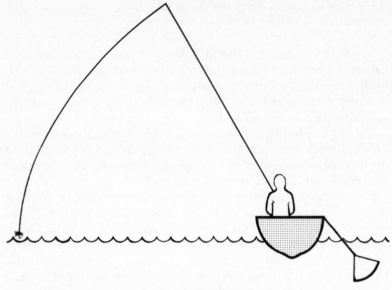

Fig. 16 Dapping

as the breeze starts to fall, raise the rod tip to get the full force of what wind there is onto the blowline. When the wind resumes, drop the rod point to keep the fly on the surface, it may skid about, but it won't lift right off. Dapping is a two handed game and requires full-time concentration to keep the fly fishing properly.

It is always worth dropping the fly in front of a riser, a trick very much easier to describe than to accomplish. Fish looking up into the surface film for their next meal have a very restricted lateral perception, they seldom move more than about 18 inches sideways to take a dapped artificial. With a rising fish running up a line that will miss your dapped fly it is always better to have a go for the fish than to leave the fly just sitting there in hope. Even a poorly presented fly skimming quickly over the head of an advancing trout may make him turn and take when the fly alights.

Natural insects

Most British fisheries allow the use of natural insects for fishing and in my view there is little point in making artificials when the natural insect is allowed. The problem lies in obtaining a sufficient quantity to last a full day's dapping – probably between 200 and 300 daddies are needed for this. With that well-known modern invention, the large, clear plastic sack, containment and transportation becomes no problem at all. Upwards of 500 daddies can be handled in one good-sized sack. With a little care the sack can be used as a bait holder in the boat from which the live insects can be extracted without the whole lot suddenly escaping. For smaller quantities a clear plastic squash bottle is ideal.

A wide gape, up-eyed, size 10 Mayfly hook is about right for holding a couple of naturals. Daddies don't last long on the hook but it helps if you hook them in the right place which is high up on the thorax. A squirt of silicone floatant on the legs will usually improve their fishing qualities in a wave.

Apart from the daddy, there are other insects that can be used for dapping. At Ladybower and Tittesworth reservoirs I have seen mayflies during June. Additionally, there are always considerable sedge hatches on the Midland reservoirs. I have never tried it myself but some enterprising person could do worse than spend a couple of warm, windy evenings in July and August having a go with live (or dead) sedges.

The Irish have the classic dapping waters and one insect they use but which is rarely seen nowadays in England is the grasshopper. Grasshoppers can also be used to increase the effectiveness of the daddy – put one of each on a hook together and see what happens!

Artificial flies

I spend more time dapping with artificial daddies than with naturals. I tie them in the style developed by Dick Walker with all the legs trailing backwards. Crane flies vary considerably both in colour and size and it pays to vary artificials accordingly. Furthermore, each fish landed will drown an artificial fly and render it useless for further fishing for several hours while it dries out. One should carry at least a dozen for a day's fishing. I don't bother with expensive floatant, a little Red Mucilin well worked into the hackles, legs and wings will float the fly quite well enough to take fish. It is a good idea to grease your artificial daddies as soon as you have tied them and then to put your flybox somewhere nice and warm to assist the grease in penetrating the feather fibres.

It is better to fish off the upwind shore from which the daddy is being blown than to fish downwind along the leeshore. Obviously, very shallow water can be fished in this way and it often pays to go into water that is too shallow or weeded for other methods to be used.

Really heavy winds in August and September usually provide the best conditions in which to take big fish on the dap. In very strong winds it may be necessary to resort to the following device. Rig the dapping fly on a dropper about a foot up from the point, and attach a fairly heavy nymph to the point itself, a size 8 Cove's Pheasant Tail is about right. The nymph acts as an anchor and will ease the problem of keeping the dap from blowing off the water. In addition, the nymph presented in this way will often catch fish itself, a more than useful bonus.

With a visible rise the safest rule is to strike hard and fast, there is always a delay in taking up the inevitable slack. It is possible that you will pull the fly out of the fish's mouth by striking before the fish has a fair hold of the fly. However, using an artificial fly you have very little time to strike before the fish will reject it and so speed is of the essence. The strike with natural insects can be rather slower.

Occasionally (and particularly when fishing with large sedge imitations such as Orgy flies, Rat-faced McDougalls and the like), the fish will attempt to drown the fly before taking it, this is usually indicated by a very powerful boil at the fly and nothing there when the strike is made. You should watch the leader acutely after the splash (which you managed not to strike) and strike as soon as it moves – a very hard game indeed.

Undoubtedly, dapping is a great deal of fun, particularly for the absolute beginner. It can also be a deadly technique at the right time and in the right place. From early August onwards I always carry a dapping rod rigged up. Being telescopic it is convenient to carry the rod fully rigged and I don't even bother to take off the reel, leader or fly between trips. I usually fish the dap as an experimental alternative to fishing wet fly. The left hand man in the boat daps while his partner shortlines a team of small wet flies with the emphasis on short range casting, figure of eight retrieving and minimum rod movement and disturbance. As soon as the dap starts to produce, out comes the other dapping rod. It is not possible for one partner to fish forwards at long range with lures and still have the dap working effectively.

5 *Northampton style*

Northampton style allows the boat fisherman to fish deep on the drift. As has been pointed out this is very difficult to accomplish from a boat drifting side-on.

There is nothing radically new about this technique. Any salmon, seatrout or downstream wet fly fisherman will be familiar with the use of sinking lines to present the fly in a current at a specific depth on a tight line swinging across the fish. The flylines used in Northampton style fishing were developed in the 1950s by river fishermen on the west coast of America. Tournament casters like Marvin Hedge and the steelhead fishermen of the Eel, Klamath and other rivers pioneered a technique of using shooting head sinking and leadcore lines. Northampton style fishing represents nothing more than the adaptation of these techniques to a stillwater scenario. The difference being that movement is generated by the boat running downwind instead of by the current of a river.

Boat control equipment

Movement of the boat and the control of that movement are the keys to successful Northampton style fishing and a variety of devices and methods have been developed to achieve this end.

The drift control rudder incorporates two main design features that differentiate it from ordinary rudders: it is large and has the capability of being set and locked into position. The reason for size is simple: the larger the area of the rudder, the greater the possible crosswind drift angle and the better the steering.

Rudder shape is also relevant to the question of steering. Normal rudders are set up with the effective area behind the shaft. A far better arrangement is to have an identical area in front of the shaft. Should one wish to run under power, however, the rudder should be modified to one third in front of the shaft and two thirds behind. The herring drifters of the North Sea in the 1930s used rudders of the same design; any more area in front of the shaft caused the rudder to flutter badly when under power. This is not a problem in drifting under wind power alone (see appendix V for details of design and manufacture).

Two further points are worth mentioning: rudder security and boat safety. A security chain prevents losing the rudder over the side. Simply drill a hole in the plate, attach a chain and fix the other end securely to the boat.

The main mistake to be made with a rudder is to run aground. Two catastrophes are possible when this occurs: either the rudder is smashed or the transom is pulled out of the back of the boat. A transom accident was the ostensible cause for the banning of rudder fishing at Grafham – in my view a regrettable move.

At Rutland, it is unnecessary to take a rudder along, the boats are provided with one. All one needs is a block of foam rubber to jam between the handle and transom.

Three other devices can be used to steer the boat bow downwind: the drogue, the chain, and locking oars. I attach a drogue to the rudder at water level. This way the drogue can be very close to the boat and the chance of getting the flies stuck in it or having fish being spooked by it are minimal.

The chain with or without ball attached is another way of achieving the same end. All one does is to lower it over the stern and regulate the speed by letting more or less out. The disadvantages are that over shallow water it may only be possible to let a little out without fouling the bottom, and this equipment does mean a lot of clutter in the back of the boat.

The oar locking yoke works by fixing the oars down the sides of the boat with their blades in the water. Different boat designs may require slight modifications to the yoke. By pulling one oar further down towards the bows and ensuring that most of the weight in the boat is concentrated in the stern it is possible to steer after a fashion.

Of these four devices, the rudder is by far the most useful as it also enables one to have a considerable degree of control over the speed of the boat. Speed can be controlled in two ways, by setting and locking the rudder at an angle or by continuously steering the boat to tack, thus 'spilling' the wind (see Fig. 18).

Drifting speed and steering

If fish are lying 12 feet down and the boat is running at 4 knots in a

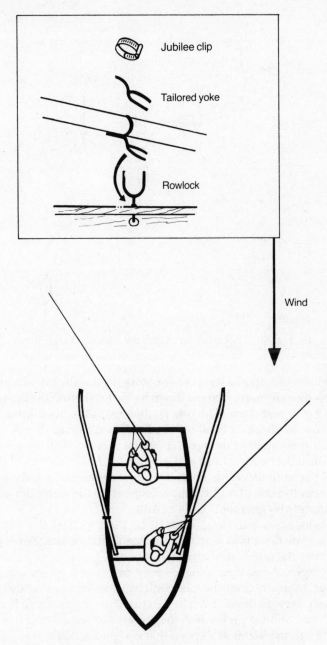

Fig. 17 Nose-down drifting: oar yoke technique

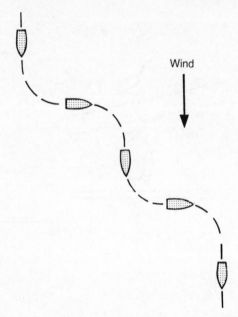

Fig. 18   Tack steering to spill the wind and slow the boat

heavy wind, then a leadcore shooting head is the only line that will
sink quickly enough to get down to the fish before the boat has run
50 yards past them. The rule is: the slower the boat drifts, the less
dense the shooting head required to fish at a given depth.

In the situation outlined above, at 2 knots drift speed a Super
Aquasink shooting head will cope and at 1 knot a Wet Cel II.

I prefer to fish from a boat drifting at between ½ and 1 knot, the
slower the rate of drift the more intensively the water can be fished.
Simply, you get more casts per drift.

In heavy wind, drogues must be used to slow the boat down.
There are three points at which a drogue may be attached to the boat
to vary the rate of downwind drift.

Obviously, several drogues may be used in combination; however, there are limits beyond which one should not go and it is certainly very inadvisable to attempt to fish in winds above Beaufort 6.

Trout show a preference: they will only take a lure if it is coming
through the water at a speed that is right for them. It is frequently
necessary to fish at a faster or slower speed than you might find

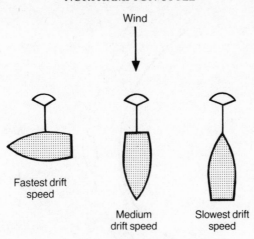

Wind

Fastest drift
speed

Medium
drift speed

Slowest drift
speed

Fig. 19   Drogue attachment positions to vary the speed of the drift for
Northampton style

comfortable. If you want to catch fish, you have to present the lure to
them in the way they want it.

Coupled with the problem of drifting the boat at an appropriate
speed is the problem of steering accurately. When commencing a
drift it is necessary to mark the position and then to remember how
the boat was steered down the drift. This is because fish lie in shoals
and if you cannot run down the line on which you took fish on the
drift before, then you will not contact the shoal on a second attempt.
A major cause of frustration is wind change: either speed or
direction. A boat steers differently under different windspeeds.
One must keep a constant weather eye on the wind and modify
one's steering to suit.

A not uncommon situation is exemplified by the problem of drifting for the packs of large brown trout that gather near the shoreline
of the East Bank of Rutland Water during late September and
October.

As indicated in the diagram, fish lie along half a mile of shoreline
holding between 60 and 90 yards out.

If you cannot steer your boat precisely to hold 75 yards offshore all
the way around the bank, then your time spent fishing into water
that holds fish is indeed limited.

A chance discovery has enabled me to get a better steering control. If the boat is steered on the wrong tack for deep fishing, the bow

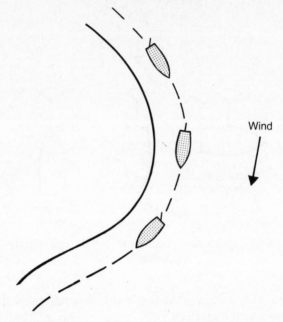

Fig. 20   Where the ability to steer pays off. Working around a bank to
cover fish lying a specific distance offshore

partner's line goes under the keel and he is rendered substantially
incapable of fishing effectively.

My then companion had the habit of steering the boat in this
manner. One day, greatly frustrated, I moved down the boat so that
I could get the point of my rod outside the stern of the boat and thus
avoid the problems. This worked and I was able to fish effectively
once more.

It became obvious, in the weeks that followed, that the boat
steered very much more precisely and was manoeuvrable at slower
speeds than had previously been possible. The effect of both
partners standing at the stern is to dig the keel in, this makes the
boat more manoeuvrable.

I now make sure that both anchors are stored near the stern of the
boat as well. It is also important to balance the weight in the boat
equally on both sides of the keel. An off-balance boat tends to turn
heavy side downwind, and steers poorly.

Ruddered boat control is an art on its own. Judgement of speed
and direction is very much more subtle than the casual onlooker

1   Anchor fishing, nose down

2   Fishing over the front: Tommy Graham casts while the author
works the bob fly

3 Boat layout for right handers fishing Northampton style

4 Left and right handers in casting positions at stern

5 Trolling with rods safely resting in the boat

6 Boat organisation for fishing nose down at anchor and stern quarter drifting

7 The fruits of good boatfishing displayed by the author and Jim Clements at Rutland Water

would ever dream. It is an essential skill in Northampton style fishing. To develop expertise evenly it is a good idea if partners take turns at the helm day about. Otherwise, the bow man may have a hard time on the helmsman's annual holiday.

Boat organisation and tackle

Plates 3 and 4 illustrate how the boat should be organised for partners who are both right handed (mirror image for left handed partners). Partners who are opposite handed use a slightly different modus operandum (Pl. 5). Both partners stand or sit closely together at the stern of the boat. Any attempt on the part of the bow man to position himself near the bows will guarantee that his partner hooks him while casting.

I use two basic tackle systems as detailed in appendix III, the heavier AFTM 12 for fishing deep and dealing with heavy winds, the lighter AFTM 9 for fishing slow sinking lines nearer the surface.

As fish lie at precise depths, it is essential that both partners use identical flylines of identical length; shooting heads should be cut from opposite ends of a double tapered line and shared between partners. Experience has revealed that differences as little as one AFTM rating between otherwise identical lines matter significantly. Even the same backing should be used.

Make sure the leader lands fully extended, if it does not then the fly will not fish effectively until the slack has been retrieved and this leads to missed opportunities on the drop and a lack of depth control for the fly. The rod must not be held at an angle to the line nor pointed up in the air; this leads either to gentle takes being missed or not felt at all. The rod should be pointed straight down the line with the tip just clear of the water. In theory this should give rise to repeated smash takes but in practice it does not. In the last decade I have experienced only seven smash takes, just one of which resulted in a line breakage. However, I do not fish with light tackle: I use a 16-foot leader of 13 lb. BS Racine Tortue for Northampton style fishing in normal conditions.

Northampton styles

There are four basic approaches to fishing from a boat in Northampton style: hold-on fishing, fishing the fall, side swiping and pitch and pay.

HOLD-ON FISHING

In hold-on fishing the fisherman pays out his flyline until the required depth is reached. Drifting nose down the wind usually implies a fairly leisurely rate of advance, compared with trolling. Therefore there is little to detract from the use of shooting heads backed onto nylon monofil.

However, monofil stretches and is not as positive a take indicator as a continuous flyline. The way I overcome this is to use a continuous line made by splicing two forward tapers together at the thin ends. Appropriate composite lines are detailed in appendix III.

It is theoretically possible to fish at any depth merely by using continuous leadline, governing the depth by the amount let out. However, this proves impractical when fishing at depths less than 20 feet because the fly will not be far enough away from the boat, particularly later in the season when the fish have had time to associate boats with trouble. Ideally, one should fish with the fly 30–70 yards behind the boat, hence the reason for carrying a wide range of sinking lines.

Another advantage of fishing a long way behind the boat is that one can, by thoughtful use of the rudder, induce a fair amount of speed variation, and this has the effect of making the fly lift and drop and also swing round on gentle curves. Very often these micro variations in the path of the fly provide the added stimuli that provoke a following fish into taking.

Hold-on fishing, like trolling, is prone to produce the extended tap take. One should not therefore strike at every little tickle, as Dick Shrive has commented, 'Sit still, do nothing; they don't know it is feathers'.

The flies and general approaches one will find effective in hold-on fishing are similar to those appropriate to trolling, and mentioned in that chapter. Any qualifications merely reflect the reduced speeds involved in hold-on fishing; the fish have longer to inspect the fly before deciding to take, so it is better to use flies at least two hook sizes smaller than you would for trolling. Also one should concentrate on using flies that might be mistaken by the fish for a natural foodform like the leech or fry. Imitation goldfish rarely work well with this style although on warm June and July days a pale yellow-winged lure with a maroon chenille body often produces spectacular if illogical success.

Hold-on fishing requires far less physical effort than the other

Northampton styles and it will take a fair number of fish. It is generally far more effective for taking rainbow trout in the upper 15 feet of the water than for brown trout which are very difficult to tempt with a one-pace retrieve.

BACKDRAGGING

Lures are used almost exclusively in hold-on fishing because of the fast boat speed in relation to the movement of the surface water. However by drifting the boat sideways its progress slows down until it is little faster than the drift of the top few inches of water. In this situation imitations of spent insects and emerging pupae dragged behind the boat give a very natural appearance and can be most effective.

This technique, known as backdragging, is mainly suited to small imitative flies. However I would recommend the occasional use of a floating Baby Doll lure on a sinking tip. This results in the Doll being dragged along just below the surface, a deadly representation of a sickly fry when the latter are high in the water.

Unfortunately, hold-on and backdragging are stultifyingly boring techniques but they remain the most effective methods for introducing beginners to boatfishing.

FISHING THE FALL

Fishing the fall or swing fishing was developed at Grafham by Dick Shrive, Bob Church and others. It relies on the boat moving relatively slowly on a sharp crosswind angle in moderate wind conditions. In light winds a sufficient speed is obtained by running pretty much straight downwind. Heavier wind conditions necessitate the use of a drogue or chain to slow the boat down to a steady rate of advance; an optimum speed is one mile per hour.

A feature of drifting across the wind is that the boat does not drift precisely down the line of the keel, it slips slightly downwind. Swing fishing relies upon the cast being made no further sideways than at right angles to the boat's actual line of travel. If one casts only one or two degrees on the downwind side, then the fly sinks slackly for a considerable part of the retrieve, instead of swinging on a tight line from the moment that it touches down.

The diagram overleaf (Fig. 21) indicates the angles at which the cast should be made.

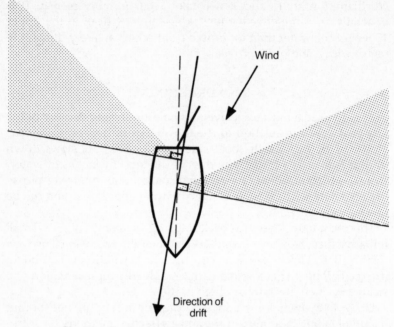

Wind

Direction of
drift

Fig 21   Casting at right angles to the line of the drift

The basic tactic in fishing the fall is to cast 25 to 35 yards sideways and then to hold on as the fly is pulled down and round; the retrieve is started only when the line straightens behind the boat and should be slow and steady.

The depth to which the fly sinks during the swing is governed by three factors: the distance cast, the density of the shooting head and the speed of the boat. The timing of the takes gives a strong clue as to the correct fishing depth. If all the takes are coming late on in the hold part of the sequence and in the first few pulls of the retrieve, it normally pays to use a denser head and to cast shorter, that way you get more fishing at the productive depth. Takes coming in the first half of the retrieve cycle indicate that the fish are higher in the water and a change to a less dense line is required.

The great flyline for this style of fishing is the Wet Cel II shooting head. Other useful lines are detailed in appendix III.

Fishing the fall can be very successful in gentle winds when it pays to use AFTM 9 or lighter shooting heads. Heavier lines are likely to spook the fish, particularly when they are feeding high in the water.

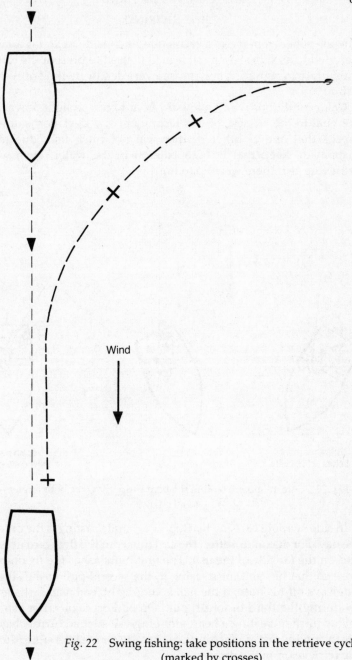

Fig. 22   Swing fishing: take positions in the retrieve cycle
(marked by crosses)

Wind

SIDE SWIPING

The all-pulled retrieve is a technique of considerable importance.
Referred to as side swiping, it is mainly used to present the lure on
the surface to rising fish and can be a very deadly method of evening
fishing.

Calm conditions which allow the boat to run straight downwind
are vital to the success of this technique; any deviation sideways
means that one or other partner will not catch fish, due to an
inability to keep the fly high enough in the water, even when
retrieving as if there were no tomorrow.

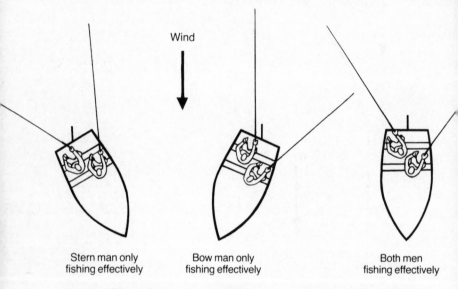

| Stern man only | Bow man only | Both men |
| fishing effectively | fishing effectively | fishing effectively |

Fig. 23 Side swiping: steering the boat properly gives both anglers an
equal chance

In side swiping to rising fish highly accurate casting is the order of
the day. For maximum effect the cast must put the fly a yard upwind
and on the far side of the fish. The first pull flashes the fly onto his
nose so that he can't miss seeing it, the second pull flashes the fly
sideways off his nose; if the fish is coming he will usually have the
fly during the third or fourth pull. On odd occasions, the fish will
follow further creating a heart-stopping vee-shaped furrow behind
the fly; pull as fast as you can and get ready for the take either during
the retrieve or on the draw.

The standard line for this style is either a slow-sinker or a sinking tip. However, on some occasions the fish respond better to a fly plunging downwards and away than one running level. To cope with this and other flights of fancy I often use a Super Aquasink shooting head which allows great flexibility in the retrieve path.

Side swiping has a place in daytime fishing, again almost always to observed risers. Normally surface feeding fish during the day are preoccupied with a specific foodform. With larger foodforms, it is generally far more profitable to turn the boat sideways on and fish over the front with a team of imitations. However, when the fish are preoccupied with smaller items, particularly those infuriating wriggling olive buzzers around hook size 20 or, even worse, when daphnia rise to the surface, fishing with natural imitations often becomes profitless. One effective way to break such preoccupations is to use shock tactics, for example sideswiping lures.

During the early part of the season far and away the best lure is a Small White Tube about 1½ inches long. As the season progresses, lure size should be decreased, the flat-winged L/S 8 Missionary is about right during late July and August. When the fish are taking pinfry, at any time from mid June until late August, the lure has to be very much smaller still: a White Rabbit Nymph, or a long shank 12 Baby Doll are about the best bets. At night time and later in the season, black is the colour to use.

PITCH AND PAY

This method was developed to deal with fish feeding at specific depths in particular between 10 and 40 feet deep in which the largest proportion of feeding fish in any eutropic stillwater is likely to be encountered.

Pitch and pay fishing is easy to accomplish, one casts a relatively short line at somewhere near right angles to the line of drift; the backing is shaken out of the rod tip and the retrieve commenced when everything tightens up.

This apparently simple technique has two major points to commend it. With the shooting head dropping under free fall it becomes possible using the stop watch to fish at a precise depth cast after cast. Use of different densities of shooting head and varying amounts of backing paid out means that this accuracy can be achieved at depths up to 40 feet; any deeper and accuracy declines; other devices have

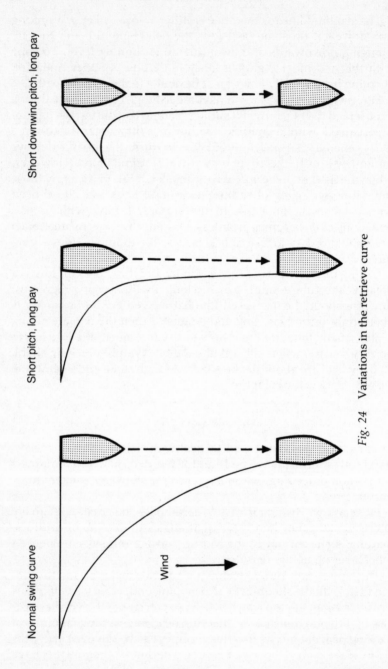

Short downwind pitch, long pay

Short pitch, long pay

Normal swing curve

Wind

Fig. 24 Variations in the retrieve curve

to be resorted to. Additionally the short cast produces a very accentuated curve in the retrieve path which often induces a take. I suspect this is because trout rarely take their prey from behind. They pursue and attack as soon as the fry makes a break to the side. Not only do they attack broadside on, they attack at the head end. Brownies hit in the front third. Rainbows sometimes hit a little further back around the middle.

With fish that are accustomed to feeding on fry, this behaviour becomes a reflex with the takes occurring as soon as the lure swings off a straight retrieve path. This curve can be further emphasised by casting so that the leader and fly extend in a straight line downwind to the line of the shooting head. Occasionally, it pays to cast in this manner to fry feeders working in shallow water using floating, sinking tip or slow sinking shooting heads depending on depth. I have had some great days fishing this way in Grafham's Savages Creek in August and September.

TARGET POPULATIONS

As noted before, pitch and pay's main application is for a population of fish feeding at a particular depth. Suspended populations can

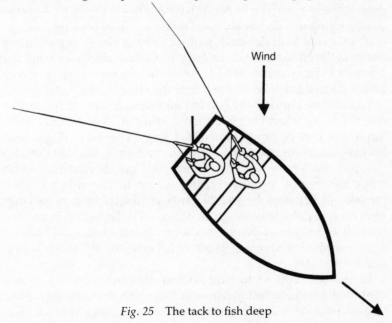

Fig. 25 The tack to fish deep

occur at any time of the season in any depth of water. Only experience of a water and a great deal of experimentation will enable the fisherman to locate those populations.

The technique's other major use is to present the fly just above the bottom. Precision bottom fishing on the drift is extremely difficult to undertake effectively and demands that the boat be tacked as illustrated. One needs to know exactly how deep the water is, right along the line of the drift, in order to fish all the bottom features correctly. This intimate knowledge can only be built up over the years as outlined previously. The ability to present one's flies very close to the bottom is essential in mid-season brown trout fishing due to the fishes' habit of lying semi-comatose on the bottom during the long hot summer days. Fishing the fly within a foot or so of their heads is often the only way of persuading such fish to have a go.

Longfall

The tactical variation of longfall fishing is the means to achieve this. In water 15–25 feet deep one can fish the bottom with the leadcored shooting head. However, in high summer this is by no means as productive as using the Super Aquasinker to get the fly to the same depth. Using this slower sinking line with a lot of backing paid out enables a very long flat-track retrieve to be made, thus presenting the fly at the effective depth for longer. Additionally in the height of summer large brownies tend to follow the fly for a very long way before deciding to take, so the longer the retrieve, the better.

You require high quality backing for this technique to reduce the risk of tangles when long lengths are paid out. I recommend 30 lb. Stren, the best currently available. Using Stren, 60 to 70 yards of backing can be dropped, in light wind conditions, without tangles.

Again, over water 25–40 feet deep you can fish the bottom by using continuous leadline, casting out up to 20 yards and then paying out between 10 and 20 yards of further lead as backing. However, for the reasons given above, it is far better to use the longfall technique of paying out a great deal of monofil backing after a leadcored shooting head so keeping the fly at the killing depth for longer.

To fish the bottom in over 40 feet of water, one has to use continuous leadline and to fish with it in much the same way. Continuous leadline is unpleasant to use in this manner: it is evil to cast, it tangles badly in the boat and it is quite difficult, due to the drag and the weight of the line itself, to detect exactly when to commence the retrieve. Also, being thin and relatively abrasive it tends to cause line burns whenever a fish takes hold. A partner once collected 18 line burns in a day!

When fish are lying deep and taking deep, retrieve only twenty yards and then pay the line out again. When fish are chasing the fly right up then retrieve to the surface, a very laborious business when fishing with 60 yards of continuous leadline.

I hate having to fish the long lead and only resort to it when conditions make it mandatory: usually during heat waves in July and August when brown trout can lie 50 and 60 feet down and often deeper.

As an alternative to using continuous leadline, I have been experimenting with composite lines. Nothing sinks as fast as long lead. However, a length of leadline coupled to the fine leadcored backing off a forward tapered Super Aquasinker is an adequate compromise. One such rig consists of a Cortland Kerboom 450 grain shooting head joined onto 75 yards of fine Super Aquasinker (cut from three forward tapers and spliced together). The head and 50 yards paid out will match the depths reached by 40 yards of long lead. A faster drop can be obtained by using 20 yards of continuous 45 lb. BS Mark V Gladding lead in front of the Super Aquasinker backing.

One fisherman I know has been using a composite line consisting largely of piano wire coupled with leadcored shooting heads sewed side by side, to produce an effect rather akin to a downrigger. The field for further experimentation with composite lines is wide open.

Microvariation

The basic problem in pitch and pay is finding the depth at which fish are feeding. The practical way is for each partner to fish with a different line until one begins to catch, after which both partners fish identically. This is not the entire picture, however.

The key to hitting the taking depth is the technique of microvariation, namely the ability to exploit the full range of depths that the line is capable of. For example, when using the Super Aquasink shooting head (it is, after all, my favourite) you can achieve a tremendous variation in depth and in action by casting different distances from the boat, at different angles, and paying out different lengths of backing. Casts can be varied from 15 yards to 35, the angle from a right angle to within about 10° of the eye of the wind and the payout from nothing up to 70 yards. In practice, one systematically varies one or more of these three factors with each cast in an attempt to fish fairly quickly through the range of the line's possibilities.

When fish start to take, one further refines the presentation by fishing the lure at the taking depth but at a variety of retrieve speeds, curves and angles on the cast until the most productive combination is found.

Highly sophisticated fishermen may use heavier or lighter lines combined with shorter or longer freefall timings to put the lure through at an identical depth but with a very different action. These secondary variations are occasionally more effective, though not often.

Catching fish

What normally happens is that you and your partner will be experimenting away for a couple of hours or so when all of a sudden a fish will take hold. The inexperienced will make little of it but this event signals the start of what may develop into what I call a sequence, a chance to take a lot of fish for a short time only.

Sequencing

Many factors affect fish feeding deep: light conditions, variations in windspeed, the time of day, food lifting off the bottom, the speed of the fly, curve on the fly, etc., too complicated usually for precise analysis. The practical thing to do is to present the lure in exactly the same way that it was presented on the successful cast. In the excitement of hooking, playing and netting the fish, the amateur will probably have forgotten the essential details: the angle and length of the cast, amount of backing out and the position of the boat at the take. All these factors must be remembered and, above all, there is a need for speed – the faster a fish is netted, the faster the fly can be got back into the water and the next fish hooked.

If a sequence has been hit and lost, never keep running the boat down the drift, there may be other shoals further on but there is no guarantee. Repeat the drift immediately and keep on until the fish stop taking, only then can you relax.

Sequencing is the key to productive deep fishing. Only rarely will both partners sequence on mid-water feeders simultaneously, probably because of light conditions; whereas fishing at depths of more than 15 feet both partners will usually manage to sequence simultaneously. The ability to fish sequences is of critical importance for specimen hunters: large fish will usually only feed in one area for a short time, one large fish hooked is the only indication that there is a pack feeding hard below you. The ability to sequence simultaneously will give you and your partner one or two chances in a season to make a truly spectacular double limit. The best that I and Jim Clements have managed has been (at Rutland, with a second ticket) 22 fish for 66 lb. 10 oz. The first 16 came between 1.30 p.m. and 5.42 p.m. from a drift 500 yards long; we ran it eight times.

It is often difficult for the newcomer to decide whether to persist with a drift line. A good guide is the rate of takes: if you and your partner are getting two takes or more every half hour then you are right to continue. Otherwise change your lines, your drift or your fishing style. This assumes that no fish are showing on the surface.

Hitting a sequence of fish early in the day can send one home early. This, to me, is a bonus; I would sooner have my busy hour and go. Frequently in the past I have deliberately experimented to break a sequence and have ended the day going home with rather less than the limit that would have come had I not been so foolish.

Trout and lures

My case for the use of lures rests on the following facts. The trout is a predator of the first rate. The rainbow in its natural surroundings in the stillwaters of North America is capable of growing into the 50 lb. class by predating almost exclusively on degenerated species of salmonids, such as the Cisco and Kokanee. Frankly, the rainbows we fish for in this country are poor runted things compared with their forebears, denied their favourite foods and dead before their time.

Brown trout and sea trout are taxonomically indivisible and I wonder whether the behaviour of brown trout in large stillwaters differs markedly from the behaviour of sea trout in the sea, where there is no insect life whatsoever and sea trout grow large and strong on a diet of crustaceans and fish. The trout's natural predilection to attack and consume other fish has been settled, in evolutionary terms, for a very long while indeed.

All these facts suggest that it makes sense to fish for trout with lures that could be taken for large natural food forms: the significant ones are fry and leech.

Lures – actions and dressings

For deep fishing, there are several other requirements that the lure has to fulfil. It has to be light and must, on no account, sink faster than the line it is being fished in conjunction with. It is difficult enough gauging depth near the bottom without being further troubled by a fly that actively seeks out weed to attach to itself. It must swim straight as no trout I know of will make a pass at a fly that fishes out of balance (other than with a controlled wobble).

The tendency for the fly to wing-wrap, either in casting or when taken and missed by a fish should also be reduced by ensuring that wing dressings do not protrude greatly past the hookbend. Unfortunately, with trout hitting the lure at the front or middle, if one dresses one's flies with the hook located at the front or the middle these flies wing-wrap.

There are distinctive actions that particular dressings incorporate. These are three-fold: single action, in which the fly fishes as an integral whole, the best example of which is the Baby Doll; double action, in which the wing hinges upwards as the fly falls and closes whenever the fly is pulled on the retrieve such as marabou tandems; and the wriggler which possesses a tail action, exemplified by the hackle winged Tube Fly. Certain authorities allege a fourth type, the hackle-pulse action obtained by using a large collar hackle on the fly. However I am dubious about this.

I feel that particular dressings work best in a specific size range; for example, I only like my Appetizers in L/S 8 and L/S 6. Hence the list of lures for Northampton style given below (the dressings are in the appendix) is large in terms of numbers of dressings. Apparent duplications reflect variations of action. For convenience I have categorised the flies in terms of basic colour.

White	*Black*	*Fancy*
White Rabbit Nymph 10	Black Chenille L/S 8,6,4	Baby Doll variations
Baby Doll L/S 12-4	Bloody Maria L/S 6	Green Back L/S 8

Appetizer L/S 8-6	J.P.S. L/S 6	Mickey Finn L/S 8
Zero	Chenille Muddler L/W 8,6,4 double	Chenille H. Muddler L/S 6, orange, fluorescent green
Missionary L/S 8-6	Christmas Tree L/S 8 tandem	Red Baron L/S 8, 6 tandem
Flatwing Missionary 10,8,6	Black Tubes	Yellow Wing L/S 8,6 maroon chenille body
White Lure L/S 8,6,4	Black Tube, fluorescent green cheeks 2–3 ins	Yellow Tubes 1¼–3 ins
White Christmas Tree tandem L/S 8,6	Murderer L/S 8 tandem	Leprechaun Matuka L/S 8 Hot Orange Tubes 1¼–3 ins
All White Tandem L/S 8,6	Black Tandem L/S 8 & 6	White/Orange Tubes 1¼–3 ins
Chenille Head Muddler L/S 8,6	Green Cheek Black tandem L/S 8,6	Flectolite Silver L/S 6 tandem
		Flectolite Copper L/S 6 tandem
White Tube 1¼–4 ins	Zuluka L/S 8,6	Flectolite Gold L/S 6 tandem
White Tube, fluorescent green cheeks 2–3 ins		
Badger Matuka L/S 8,6		

One has to match the action of the fly to the style being fished. The use of flies with pronounced actions of the wriggler type is not recommended for hold-on style, due to the likelihood that they will get wrapped up by a tap taker. In fishing by casting and retrieving with frequent opportunities to examine the fly, the wriggler type of fly can be used.

Almost every fly detailed also has a fluorescent variation. Inexplicably on some days, months and even whole seasons, the fish prefer a fluorescent variation. The inclusion of fluorescent materials, particularly lime-green wool, makes the fly very much more visible in the water to human eyes; they are also probably more visible to the trout.

All waters fish differently to the lure from time to time, so it is not possible to lay down specific patterns peculiar to a water. Also the effectiveness of particular lures changes from season to season: a good lure last year is unlikely to remain one for all time. Oddly, a season tends to settle itself around a specific lure; if you can find a lure that works well for the first two months of a season, do not change to something else in a hurry.

The general rule is that when fishing deep the larger flies are more effective than the smaller, fishing near the surface the smaller sizes outfish the larger.

Orange flies have always struck me as being somewhat unsporting in that I cannot fit them into my philosophy about representing fry or leech. Why trout take them is a mystery. But, if it is August and bright and windy, and there are rainbows about, hot-orange may well outfish everything.

The more I fish the more I realise how very little I know about the fundamental reasons why fish prefer one lure to another. I advise you only to ensure that you fish with different flies from your partner and experiment. If your partner discovers the solution, change over immediately, experiment no longer, time may be short.

Coda

It is as easy to become obsessively attached to Northampton style as to any other. On the Midlands reservoirs it will produce fish on seventy per cent of all fishing days. It has its limitations. First, it is not particularly effective when fish are feeding high in the water on insects.

Secondly, fish in the upper strata can refuse to take a fly swinging across the wind. The undoubted cause of this is the effect of surface drift in the topwater. Usually these fish will take the lure only when it is travelling straight upwind: stern quarter droguing is the answer.

Thirdly, there are always odd days between the start of June and the end of September when trout will just not take a fly larger than a size 12. Why, I know not. The remedy is to anchor up and fish deep with nymphs or to fish over the front. The difficulty lies in identifying whether it is a small fly day or not. If you fish for the first five hours or so for no takes to the lure, it may well be one!

Fourthly, at times trout gather in a particular area, usually close inshore, leaving the main water virtually devoid of feeding fish. There are, also, the rough-water packing situations near stain as noted previously. When fish are in a static shoal, it is sensible to sit quietly at anchor and pick them off as they cruise around their beat.

With these provisos, Northampton styles are to be commended on any water in the U.K. They are much more subtle in practice than can be explained on paper, and the beginner is further warned that it will take four or more seasons to master these methods. They are specialist tools indeed.

6 *Trolling*

Trolling, fishing by letting the flies out of the stern of the boat and rowing them around the water, is very little talked about either publicly or privately. There is a considerable stigma attached to trolling amongst fly fishermen, most of whom appear to regard it as being indistinguishable from cheating. That is unjustified because many waters have designated areas in which trolling under power of oars is allowed, and one should not feel guilty about using the method when conditions are appropriate. Trolling, like all other methods of boat fishing, is highly effective when the conditions are favourable and worse than hopeless when they are not. Unfortunately the best conditions for trolling also tend to favour other more interesting and less tiring methods.

Trolling enables flies or lures to be presented at a precise depth and at precise speeds; it is the only means of making a very long continuous upwind retrieve.

On most of the fisheries that permit trolling, the trolling areas are set out over deep water; which means that for large parts of the season they are almost fishless, except following a heavy stocking. Undoubtedly, such areas contain numbers of large deep lying fish but these are difficult to contact as with oar powered trolling it is almost impossible to guarantee continuous speed of the boat and, therefore, to present the fly the necessary few inches off the bottom or precisely along the thermocline. The most productive areas for trolling are the shallower parts holding most fish where trolling is usually banned; trolling under motor power to enable the depth of the fly to be regulated precisely is also banned.

So what are the best conditions for trolling? If you are fishing with a pulling boat, in an area in which trolling is permitted, then it makes sense to troll whilst rowing back up the wind. It also makes sense to troll even by rowing a motor boat back upwind in such an area, but only when the fish are showing no interest whatsoever in a pulled retrieve but are willing to take the fly when fished on the swing or held-on. These tend to be days on which only rainbows feed. It is also worth rowing across a trolling area late on in the evening when large brown trout sometimes show an interest in a large black or white lure trolled within a few feet of the surface.

As you may have gathered, I troll very rarely as I find it rather uninteresting. Despite its limited attraction there are right and wrong ways to set about it, and trolling properly is not quite as simple as the casual observer might think.

The only item of equipment crucial for successful trolling is the reel. There are two major features that make a good trolling reel: an adjustable drag and the capability to run silently. When trolling it is not sufficient to secure one's line by either wrapping it once round the reel seat or relying on the check of the reel. The former method frequently causes the hook to be torn out or your leader to be smashed. The open reel technique usually ensures that the hook doesn't go in properly and unsettles the fish which follows the fly and gives it occasional knocks prior (hopefully!) to taking a firm hold. Using a reel equipped with a satisfactory drag it is a very simple matter to set the drag so that it will hook a fish and give line if the beast pulls hard. The reason for silent running is twofold: first, to be truly silent a reel has to run smoothly under drag and this indicates that the drag setting can be made precisely; the other reason is the obvious one: lack of noise. Oddly, many fishermen are not aware of the fact that under certain atmospheric conditions sound travels very well over water, particularly in an upwind direction. There is no bigger giveaway than the noise of a fish running on the reel: in adverse flat-calm conditions, it can attract fishermen from over a mile – enough said!

As in all other forms of fishing from boats, the organisation of the boat is of considerable importance and the photograph (Pl. 5) shows the way to organise a boat for trolling.

Certain features are worthy of note. Firstly, there are no impediments, such as the rudder, hanging in the water over the back of the boat. This makes rowing as easy as possible.

The lucky fellow not rowing sits at the bow end not only to superintend the tackle but also to hold the bow down. It is easier to row into the wind with weight in the bows; the boat spends less time going up and down and more time going forwards.

Trolling is a genuine test of partnership. The man in the bow not only has the pleasure of managing the tackle but also lands the fish, the oarsman has the mundane role of boat mover, general dogsbody and netsman. Naturally, both partners share the rowing and the chances to land the fish.

Jim Clements and I follow a set routine when trolling and as we divide the bag, it really doesn't matter who does what.

The oarsman gets underway and the bow man casts his gear out over the right hand side of the boat, pays out the line, locks his reel and passes the butt of his rod under the oarsman's right arm feeding the rod back until the reel can be dropped over the bow seat. Simultaneously, the oarsman gets his gear over the left hand side and then passes the rod back under his left arm. The bow man pays the line off the left hand rod, locks the reel and positions the butt of the rod, reel downwards over the bow seat. Both rods have their tips inside the boat. Both reels after locking are positioned so that they are about an inch behind the seat and the first indication that a fish has taken the fly is the thump of the reel hitting the back edge of the bow seat.

With a clutched reel there is no point in panicking when a fish is hooked; the oarsman merely turns the boat until it is broadside onto the wind and ships his oars. The bow man then plays the fish out whilst the oarsman retrieves the other gear and prepares to net the fish. With the fish successfully boated the oarsman gets the boat moving again, and the cycle is repeated.

When trolling it is better not to strike. The characteristic take of the rainbow when trolling consists of a number of gentle taps and then a wallop. Any additional movement of the fly whilst this business is going on tends to be very counter-productive and certainly striking at every tap is a waste of time. Bigger rainbows and most brownies normally come just once at the fly; they either have it hard or the hooks don't go in and the only way you can influence the outcome is to have very sharp hooks indeed!

When hooked, a trolled fish tends to behave rather like a dog on a lead; after a few initial bumpings about it will allow itself to be dragged smoothly along with little resistance. In rough enough waves, I am sure that a good dragging along tends to get the fish rather drunk with oxygen. Many years ago, Ron Burgin and I were rowing away from the dam at Grafham in a heavy south-west wind with the intention of sheltering up by the Fishing Lodge; passing the end of the Sludge Lagoons, we had the misfortune to hook a very large rainbow; to get leeway to play the beast we were forced to row right into the middle of the moored yachts some 400 yards away, which took about twenty minutes in the wind and the wave. Ron wound the fish in easily and it came groggily towards the net but sobered up very quickly at the sight of yours truly; by the time we managed to boat the beggar we had the same row to do all over again; no more lines in the water that day!

The technical aspects of trolling are concerned with identifying the killing fly and determining the depth and speed at which it will be effective.

Of these three variables, speed is far and away the easiest to sort out. Even sharing the rowing, it means an awful lot of hard work. So row as slowly and steadily as you can, you won't catch any more fish practising for the Diamond Sculls than you will by just mooching steadily up the wind.

When trolling in conjunction with drift fishing use the same gear that is used in catching fish in Northampton style but follow one simple rule; Parton's rule of one line more. This relies on the fact that before you start rowing back up the wind, you will already have established roughly at what depth the fish are feeding. Basically, the trolling action of a shooting head backed to nylon monofil will put that line through the water rather higher than by fishing in Northampton style. So, with shooting heads follow the one line more rule i.e. fish with a sinking tip, troll with a Wet Cel II; fish with a Wet Cel II, troll with the Super Aquasink; fish the Super Aquasink, troll with a lead-cored shooting head. This rule breaks down at both ends of the spectrum: with surface fishing and on the days when you have to fish with a leadcored shooting head. Never be afraid to troll steadily with three small flies on a floating line if you can see fish rising. Surprising things can happen. For example, many years ago four of us were fishing at Eyebrook and as my partner and I were rowing back past our friends, a fish took hold of one of our flies and we landed it. Enlivened by this sight, our friends hurled their gear out and started rowing towards us trolling no less than six red buzzers between them on floating lines. All of a sudden, there was a despairing wail and we looked up to watch a brand new Superlite, with Mitchell Automatic and Longbelly attached, fly like a javelin over the stern of their boat, land in the water and then take on the aspect of a giant antenna float, pulling sideways whenever the fish attached to the other end tried to dive. After much rowing, cursing and groping they retrieved the rod and managed to land the 15 oz. rainbow responsible. Whatever you troll with, make certain that the gear can't shoot over the back of the boat, I know at least three people who have lost expensive carbon-fibre rods, plus attendant reels and lines, while trolling casually with small flies.

To troll back upwind when fish are being taken with the leadcored shooting head on the down drift requires a continuous leadline. I advocate the use of a metred continuous lead of the Gladding Mark

V type coloured differently every ten yards to enable one to judge precisely how much line is in the water and, therefore, to set the depth fairly accurately. I carry a hundred yards but have only once caught fish with more than fifty yards (five colours) out whilst trolling. Very deep lying fish can usually be taken with four colours out as this keeps the fly between thirty and forty feet down depending upon how fast you row. It is rarely worth fishing any deeper unless you are under power and running with the full range of American accessories (see later) to keep the fly dead over the bottom.

In theory you only need continuous leadline for trolling as you could cover all depths by letting out more or less as occasion demands and, in practice, I have trolled successfully with as little as two yards in the water. When doing this, it pays to lengthen your leader radically up to as much as twenty yards. Obviously this helps to keep the fly well away from the boat and because no casting is involved such a length can be managed fairly easily. For my own part I have never tried a leader longer than fifteen yards, but then I don't troll very much.

When I used to troll at Grafham I started off on the assumption that the more line one let out, the deeper the fly would fish. In fact, the more line we let out the less fish we caught. The reasons were twofold. Firstly, the more monofil in the water the greater the lift generated and beyond a certain length, the lift overcomes the sink and the lot starts coming up. Secondly, the more the monofil, the bigger the belly the fish has to straighten before there is much chance of the hook going in. To regulate depth use the full range of lines and never let more than about 30 yards of monofil out after the head.

There are two important design features critical to the effectiveness of trolling flies. The fly must be dressed to run smoothly and level in the water; reject any poorly tied fly that might behave like a propellor. Also, for the reasons given in connection with hold-on fishing avoid flies that can be wrapped up by the take of a fish such as hackle-winged Matukas, tube flies with forward rigged hooks and single, tandem and three hook rigs winged over-long with hair, feather or marabou. One way of overcoming this problem is to dress the flies on 4x or 6x longshank hooks with relatively short wings, extending only as far as the bend.

As for trolling patterns, these should be the same as listed for Northampton style but generally can be a couple of hook sizes larger.

Track variations

There are various ways in which the boat can be manipulated to increase the chances of taking fish. All of these cause the fly to travel in a curve and so make use of the induction theory mentioned in connection with Northampton style. They include:

(1) Rowing in a series of 'tacks' up the wind, taking care never to turn the boat too sharply as this can lead to tangles.
(2) Changing over, which takes maybe a minute to accomplish as bowman and oarsman swap positions and responsibilities. During this time the boat slows and the fly falls; as soon as rowing restarts, the fly lifts up in the water. Takes are likely to occur in the first few strokes after changeover.
(3) Rowing on a figure of 8 track and changing over every five minutes or so. Additionally, instead of making a beeline for the head of the drift, where the rules permit, try rowing around, over and across shoalwater, pipelines, old hedge lines, aerator boils and around structures.

Very occasionally, it will be a day for the trolled pulsed retrieve. This is accomplished by the bowman holding the line between the buttring and the reel and pumping a yard or so of line in and out all or part of the way up the drift. The additional spurt movement of the fly can sometimes provoke a following fish into having a go, particularly if that fish happens to be a brownie.

North American techniques

In North America, trolling for gamefish on stillwaters is a way of life. They do their trolling under motor power and use appropriate tackle.

Most of the accessory devices used in American deepwater trolling are banned from use in this country; not in specific terms but in that most waters outlaw attachments to one's flyline when fishing. However, the devices themselves are worthy of mention as they underline the principles of deepwater trolling.

Plugs, spoons, spinners or whatever are not just lowered over the back of the boat and paid out for evermore until an appropriate depth is reached. Instead, lures are rigged to a boom that can be set to run at a precise depth below the stern of the boat; when a fish takes, the tackle breaks away from the boom and the fish is played out in the usual manner.

Depth regulation can be achieved in another way; like ourselves the Americans have taken to using saltwater leadcored trolling line on stillwaters, except that they use it for trolling under power. The latest application of this method has taken place in the massive reservoirs of the West Coast States where transplanted strains of Florida largemouth bass grow to more than 20 lb. Not content with a mere 100 yards of leadline, some fishermen have been obtaining good results by splicing two reels of the stuff together. Success has been reported at speeds of around 2 m.p.h. with 14 colours (or 140 yards) of leadline paid out which must mean a fishing depth of around 100 feet as near as I can judge. Roller-ringed 4/0 sea rods and multipliers are the order of the day.

Trolling at great depth where there is little transmitted light brings another factor into play – vibration. Large predatory fish (like the rainbows of up to 56 lb. in their natural habitat of the deep lakes of North America) can be attracted by vibration. Fifty years ago, Negley Farson recommended attaching a brightly polished aluminium cooking plate some 40 feet up from the fly to create a satisfactory 'attractor' when trolling in British Columbia for rainbows and salmon. Late on in the 1980 season at Rutland I successfully hooked and landed a 10 gram copper Toby spoon from deep water near the dam; somebody else must have read Negley's book!

From my research into American practice, it seems that vibrating baits are much more effective than flies for very deep trolling. With its highly sensitive lateral line, a trout is, undoubtedly, a hunter by sound as well as sight when feeding deep; many of the lures used are specifically designed to take advantage of the trout's response to vibration patterns. Even shoal-vibration-effects can be generated by using a number of small Toby type lures without hooks set on paternoster rigs a short way in front of the lure with hooks.

A considerable amount of angling literature in the States is devoted to an analysis of the relationship between water temperature/depth/fish preferences with particular reference to the thermocline. Brown trout fishermen on Lake Michigan, for instance, take large numbers of fish, 5 lb. plus, in the summer months trolling over a mile offshore at depths of between 50 and 80 feet. They regulate the depth of fishing by measuring temperature with a thermocouple thermometer set on a boom.

The echo sounder is also used in connection with 'dan buoys', the technique being to seek out shelves, shoalwater and interesting bottom features, and to throw out buoys at appropriate places to mark the 'alley' to troll along. Possibly this technique is viable on our waters; it would certainly help anybody wishing to troll along the pipeline at Grafham!

Outrigger paravanes are used in conjunction with the downrigger boom to prevent nasty tangles. These paravanes are flown like kites in the water and will take the line well away from the area of disturbance caused by the motor around the back of the boat. The last one I saw advertised claimed to be able (at 5 m.p.h.) to support a 1½ lb. downrigger boom and then run up to 150 feet wide of the boat.

Anybody wishing to keep up to date with American practice in these interesting areas should make a point of reading Field & Stream magazine regularly.

Obviously, all these devices are relevant to the British stillwater fisherman, but only usually when on holiday in the lakes of Ireland or the lochs of Scotland where trolling under power is an accepted method of fishing. They have limited application on our reservoirs

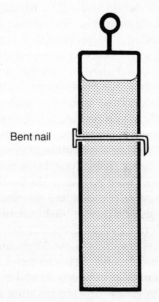

Bent nail

Fig. 26   Lead filled tubular downrigger

but the downrigger principle certainly can be used, should the rules of your water permit it. Use a shooting head made of 10 yards of AFTM 10 level neutral line and a downrigger as detailed in Fig. 26.

One casts out, pays out 20 yards of backing and then loops the downrigger hook over the mono. Next a little rope attached to the downrigger is lowered into the water and the depth is regulated by the amount of rope let out. Due to its weight the downrigger hangs straight down into the water. When a fish is hooked all one does is to give the downrigger rope a sharp upward tug and the line comes free.

Cheating

Trolling probably accounts for at least two thirds of all illegal fishing undertaken on British stillwaters. The following comments are made to enlighten the honest fisherman in what can be happening around him in the hope that he will take action by either reporting the matter or driving his boat directly across the stern of an illegal troller and cutting the line away.

When I first started fishing at Grafham, I did most of my learning (in the absence of this text book!) by following and observing well-known fishermen. One day in September I was watching a pair taking fish off the run into Savages Creek, a mild north easterly was blowing. Time and again, they rowed offshore, turned their boat round to drift back in and, within a couple of chucks, had a fish on. After this had happened about a dozen times, the penny dropped. They were cheating; trolling outside the designated area. When they hooked a fish they just kept on rowing to the head of the drift, where they turned the boat round, picked up another rod and waved it about a bit, waited for a minute, picked up the trolling rod and pretended to strike into a fish. They certainly fooled me for a while. I wonder whether they fooled themselves into thinking that they were other than cheats, both to themselves and their fellow anglers.

Unnatural behaviour usually gives cheats away. Look for boats keeping well clear of other boats and moving at half speed when they could go at full throttle, sudden movement for no good reason (except maybe to stop a rod going over the side), and parties who suddenly stop driving up the wind and start drifting from an unlikely point.

Summary

Please remember my initial comment that when conditions are favourable for trolling they are also likely to be favourable for more interesting and productive methods. For this reason, I regard trolling as an adjunct to serious fishing only, and could never advise any serious stillwater fisherman to spend more than a small fraction of his time engaged in it. After an hour, it is so boring,

7 Through the Season

The early boats – March and April

In March and April it is a great mistake to boat fish a large water by going over the front and fishing the surface layer with small flies. This is because most of the food available to the fish is lying deep and moving sluggishly. Never expect the fish to be where the food is not. Even a heavy early season buzzer hatch frequently finds the fish cruising just above the bottom, picking off the pupae as they begin their journey to the surface. Basically, one must fish deep.

A major problem in early fishing is how to avoid rainbows in spawning condition i.e. 'black' fish. Black rainbows are attracted by running water and gravel or stone bottoms. Also, they tend to run inshore, not offshore. To avoid black rainbows keep clear of shorelines and water inlets, be they streams, ditches, dykes or infall pumping pipes. Oddly, recovered silver fish can usually be found a short distance further out than black fish and it is not at all uncommon for an anchored boat sixty yards offshore to be taking bright fish whilst bank fishermen are taking black fish. A bitter winter followed by a bitter spring with the opening water temperatures never reaching 40°F usually results in all the rainbows being black in any event; this can be a tragedy if there are no brownies on the move.

Early on in the season, fish will be taken in places that they do not frequent at any other time. Every water has its own peculiarities in this respect and there are few principles which apply generally. However, one thing is fairly certain, the fish are unlikely to be down deep a long way offshore. Because of this confine your fishing to water between 10 and 40 feet deep. This implies working from onshore to offshore at the windward side or from offshore to onshore on the lee. Except where there are shoals, such as at Draycote, the fish will rarely be more than 200 yards out from the shore. Given the option, I prefer to work in towards a leeshore unless there is a heavy wind in excess of Beaufort 4.

The technique I normally employ is to drift down the wind on the rudder and to work a sawtooth search pattern until fish are located. Normally this involves one partner using a leadcored shooting head and the other a Super Aquasink shooting head. One line will be more productive than the other depending upon the day. Use the short pitch and long payout method, because early on in the season the need is to get the fly down to the fish; there is little point in slowing the fall by swing fishing.

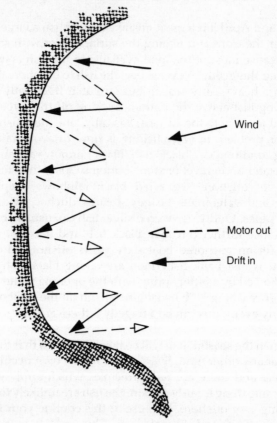

Fig. 27 Sawtooth drift pattern searching the leeshore

There are probably only 4 lures required for fishing deep early on: a 2½″ White tube, a tandem White Christmas Tree on L/S 8's, a 2½″ Black tube and a tandem Black Christmas Tree on L/S 8's.

Sooner or later one will hit a shoal of fish whilst drifting. If they are of a takeable nature (if not, move elsewhere) one has two options. You can either anchor on the shoal, nose-down style preferably; or, by careful motoring to avoid disturbance, run repeated drifts down the same line having marked that line very accurately as the shoals will be tightly packed.

Very occasionally, rainbows will be feeding on daphnia, so always spoon your fish to check if this is happening. In early spring the daphnia, which look like bright green slurry when spooned, yo-yo up and down in the water during the day. Because of this fish the same water in the same style as outlined above but extend the range of lines upwards: Sink Tip, Slow Sinker, Wet Cel II and Super Aquasink shooting heads and be prepared to change up and down when you lose contact with the fish as they follow the daphnia. Change the lures too down to L/S 8 and 6 singles; the Appetizer, Tadpoles, Black Chenille, Black and Silver and Whisky Flies are the appropriate lures, the latter two being really effective only in sunlight.

The fish will often be active in patches during the day and are particularly likely to go off the boil between 3 and 5 p.m. Evening normally heralds the start of some kind of activity, often related to the emergence of staggering quantities of black buzzers on the waters I fish. In the evening activity period, one has three options and should be well prepared to fish all of them before the fun starts.

The first to try, especially if fish are rising hard, is to fish over the front with a team of three. In a Black Buzzer rise use a Black Buzzer pupa point fly, a Grey or Brown pupa as the middle dropper and a hackled or winged black wetfly as the top dropper, Teal and Black, Blae and Black, Black Pennel or a Zulu, any will do if it is much the same size as the hatched adult. Grease is rarely called for early on, keep the flies up by pulling quickly instead.

The second option is either fishing a single black or white lure forward at risers or sideswiping and pulling very fast indeed; use the sinking tip shooting head.

The last way is to use large lures on the lead or Super Aquasink shooting heads in Northampton style. This often pays off during a sparse rise on the surface, in which the fish cannot be tempted by the methods outlined above, and which usually indicates intense activity at depth. Big lures, fished deep and fast, will often deal very adequately with this situation.

Apart from the slaughter of the innocents in the first few days of the season, early boatfishing can be patchy. Certain conditions will stop the fish feeding altogether. I fished at Pitsford in 1974 when it snowed; the Saturday before I had six fish, the Saturday after, ten; on the day it snowed not one pull all day. You pay your money and take your chances early on.

Whatever else you do, wrap up properly, take plenty of hot coffee and if the weather becomes truly atrocious, pull out and go home. It's pointless to give yourself pneumonia and a severe case of rheumatism can blight the next few weekends.

Fishing in May

Subject to the weather, the month of May can be the most productive of the entire season for boat fishermen on public waters. The stock of fish in the water is generally high; overwintered large fish have lost much of their caution; and if the weather begins to warm up, the fish are active all day long.

Fishing is radically affected by the weather, and although ambient temperatures are rising, the first two thirds of the month can be cold and unpleasant for fishing. Indeed in seven out of the last ten seasons cold north winds have prevailed until late in the month or into June before the normal south westerlies have taken over.

So, how do you fish the big cold winds and catch fish? The key word is 'work'. All day you have to work despite the fact that your hands and feet get cold, despite the wind knocking seven bells out of you and despite the tangles, the wet, the waves breaking into the boat and all the other horrors that beset you. If you give up you are lost.

Pitch and pay style with leadcored and Super Aquasinker shooting heads is the basic tactic, as in the first two months of the season. In any heavy winds, droguing the boat to let the line sink is a far more productive tactic than fishing with continuous leadline and the boat running very quickly. Tactics are pretty simple, with the boat slowed off you pitch the lead short (you won't get it far into a 20 knot wind) and pay off backing until you start occasionally hitting the bottom. The fish are generally hard on the bottom in between 15 and 35 feet and this should give a clue where to fish. At Rutland concentrate on the North and South Arms. At Grafham it tends to be more effective to fish over water up to 45 feet deep. The best early areas are along the North Shore, 40 to 100 yards off the Aeration

Tower right along to and round the Dam. Savages and the S. Buoy shoals rarely produce well until later on in the season.

You must drift the boat and keep on drifting despite the temptation to drop anchor. At this time of the season it is possible for the very good, or the very lucky, to take reasonable catches at anchor. The odds against this are high, unless you can find a nice bit of muddied leeshore water some 60 yards or so out or a pack of very gullible browns somewhere on the upwind side, which is unlikely.

The best tactic is to keep on running the boat, casting out, paying out backing and pulling in. What you do then is to run a series of different lines from the upwind shore out into the reservoir, stopping and turning back when you judge that the wave has become too savage. Sooner or later you will have a take or maybe a fish, usually you will get the take in the first four or five pulls of the retrieve. When you have had a take, mark the spot by rough triangulation (early on the fish lie in definite patches on the bottom) and run over the same area again and keep on doing it until the fish stop taking the fly. Usually you will get three or four productive drifts before the pulls stop. After two blank runs, move on.

During the course of the day you may hit, say, three taking spots. After you have worked each dry, go back to the first run and work it again, then the second productive run and then the third. In other words, keep resting the ground and then fishing it again. Very few people appreciate how small the areas of activity downstairs are. Often the only taking area in a mile of water will be 40 yards square.

The tactics above work very well on the upwind side. However, it is possible to take fish out of a mountainous wave on the leeshore, and to do this you need a slight modification to tactics. First, you dispense with the drogue and run the boat with the rudder almost locked off. Secondly, you shorten your backing from the 40 yards you will probably need to fish deep off the upwind shore, down to maybe 25 yards. A fast running boat coupled with the very worst fishing conditions makes casting almost impossible. To combat this fish mainly in castless pitch and pay style, leaving the head and backing to stream out at the end of each retrieve. Try holding on every fifth or sixth drift or so just to see if they will take a lure being dragged steadily behind the boat. Very rough waves will always bring some fish up off the bottom. They tend to feed hard and will hang in the water below the worst wave effects, around 15 feet down under a 3 foot wave. To get your lure down when running the boat as described above, a leadcored shooting head is essential; any lighter sinking line, even a Super Aquasink, just will not penetrate violent waves. You can generally pick up fish from 300 yards off the leeshore to the start of the coffee-coloured beaten up water. Don't bother fishing clouded water down deep, you will but rarely take a fish in the soup. The main band of fish will be feeding in the 100 yards upwind of the heavily coloured water.

If your water holds any concentration of rainbows you can expect them at times to feed hard on any daphnia which make a showing during the month. In cold conditions, apply the same tactics as outlined for March and April. In warmer conditions the daphnia can pose a very difficult problem during May and spasmodically throughout the remainder of the season by coming right into the surface film. Fish which become preoccupied with mopping up surface daphnia will not normally be taken by forward fishing with small flies.

The only generally effective tactics to deal with this are shock tactics; induction by the use of white lures or surface White Muddler fishing. Sideswiping sub-surface lures is one option, the other being to turn the boat sideways and to fish over the front with a greased White Muddler. At this time of year it is essential for presentation to be accurate and fishermen with highly developed casting skills, able to drop the fly within a yard of the target at 30 yards range, are at a major advantage.

On the waters that I fish, May is the month of the olive buzzer wherever conditions permit its hatching. At times the Rutland hatches are so colossal that myriads of adults can be seen dancing like columns of bonfire smoke in the lee of the Lax Hill trees in the evenings. Daytime hatches of the olive buzzer are no problem to imitate or cope with and forward fishing with a team of three fairly rough approximations should catch all the fish one needs. The evenings pose another specific problem, the return of the adult buzzers to lay eggs. There is no more difficult rise than the pre-occupation rise to adult laying buzzers. In May, the sheer quantity of available flies is often such as to render the artificial useless unless presented precisely in front of a rising fish. Even then, it often fails whilst there is sufficient light for the fish to see the weltering throngs of naturals.

At the tail end of such a rise it often pays to apply shock tactics especially as the light is going out. A small Black lure fished forward on a sink-tip shooting head may take a fish or two, often it will do rather better.

Evenings can be cold and windy throughout May and well into June. Even when the wind dies down in the last hour it is usually far better to persist with the leadline unless the air begins to feel positively warm, a rare occurrence indeed after a cold and windy day. As the evening lengthens, fish running and feeding at around thirty feet will lift up or drop down so keep a close check on fishing depth.

To summarise: the bigger fish will hold very deep for most of May. Rainbows can be found deep in the cold but might run higher if there is daphnia in the water. Spectacular rises can take place on warm days. Evenings, except when warm, are best dealt with by deep fishing. Not an easy month to fish in terms of conditions but you can rest assured that the fish are always feeding hard somewhere.

Mid-season

In June, July and August opportunities will arise to take fish by using the full range of tactical possibilities. Frequently, one has to switch methods several times during the day, to cope with this variety of trout feeding behaviour. One of my best day's fishing occurred in late July 1974 at Grafham when I took ten fish (9 middleweight rainbows and a 4 lb. 2 oz. brown) using six different techniques. That day, the fish were doing everything in rotation, starting on the surface, going down at 10.30 a.m. coming up to just under the surface at 1 p.m., dropping gradually deeper to 5 p.m. when they went off altogether until 9 p.m. For the last half hour they were feeding on adult sedge on the surface.

I find late June to be one of the hardest times of the year to take fish consistently. This could be due to defective stocking policies. However, the extreme length of daylight hours is more likely to be the cause of the problem; that and the onset of night feeding. On all the waters that I fish, night feeding becomes a marked feature in the behaviour of large brown trout starting sometime in June and finishing late on in September. When the night feeding sequence fades, predawn feeding becomes increasingly emphasised. The rainbow seems to show no such preference for night feeding and can be relied upon to produce the bulk of the midseason sport, particularly for the fisherman operating high in the water.

With the gradual deterioration of brown trout fishing for larger fish, two other target populations of fish govern the fishing, rainbows and small brown trout.

Brown trout up to around the 1½ lb. mark seem to have little taste for night cycle feeding; that or they are keen on feeding hard all day and night long.

Both these populations of fish have slightly different preferences in terms of feeding depth, the smaller browns having a great love of feeding at considerable depths during the day before coming up into the topwater in the last hour or two of daylight; the rainbow alternates between midwater and topwater feeding, again tending to become active in the topwater in the last hours before dark.

The similarity between these populations is that feeding behaviours change abruptly during the day. There is no gradual slowing down in the rate at which takes occur, just an immediate absence as the shoal switches from feeding in one mode to another; or suddenly stops altogether. The fish go off and on as if someone somewhere has turned a switch. Fishing over the Rutland deeps one July day in 1980, I had taken just one fish between 8.30 a.m. and 7.45 p.m., my partner was blank, we had had only three takes between us and there seemed no prospect of catching anything else; quite suddenly a huge shoal of browns around the 1 lb. 6 oz. mark rose up in the water and started to feed. By 8.30 p.m. we had fourteen fish in the boat and were forced to go specimen hunting to avoid having to go in early.

Dealing with abrupt switches in fish behaviour is one of the hardest aspects of boatfishing. It is all too easy to fall into a fishing routine. Having started off the day fishing in one style it takes a major act of will to reorganise the boat for fishing in an entirely different pattern.

In the midseason months, the stereotyped approach to boatfishing is fatal to obtaining consistent results, the will to change styles must exist. The typical midseason day should be thought of as having three phases, morning afternoon and evening. No matter what style is being used, the behaviour and preferences of fish will vary during the day roughly in line with the divisions outlined and one should be prepared for likely changes.

It is essential to ensure that two sets of tackle are immediately available for use, the standby being for over the front fishing; such a rod should be set up early on in the day and stored somewhere convenient to hand. When motoring out from the boathouse, I set mine up leaving the droppers empty as I prefer to put on appropriate flies immediately before fishing; I rather resent having to cut off wrong flies put on earlier as it wastes time. To prevent tangles, put on a point fly and hook it into the keeper.

In the morning, there are usually two options open, surface or deep. Quite frequently, one will start out fishing to risers and these can usually be dealt with either with small flies or by sideswiping small white lures. The deep fishing options usually involve getting the fly down to around 15 feet with a Super Aquasink shooting head fished in Northampton style, white lures tending to be the order of the day.

Should a sequence be encountered during the morning, it is unlikely to last for more than an hour.

At Grafham and Eyebrook, unlike Rutland, Pitsford and Draycote, it rarely pays to start fishing much before 10 a.m. as the fish in those waters only really wake up with the wind that seems to spring up around that time. It certainly is profitable to make an early start at Rutland as there are always a few fish moving high in the water until around 11.30 a.m. As the sun lifts, the wind establishes itself, the day starts to warm up and a change of pace sets in with the fish. Should the fish be running high by 1 p.m. it is likely that they will continue to do so for the rest of the day. Observed risers generally indicate that the day has become a small fly day, and that the lure fishing tackle can be safely put away.

Where there are no observed risers, it generally pays to fish Northampton style with the lure. In midseason the fish can be anywhere in the afternoons, from a few inches to 40 feet down. In addition, they will vary their depth as the afternoon wears on, going up or down and often yo-yoing. To cope with this one needs to use the full range of microvariation options open with sink tip, slow-sinker, Wet Cel II and Super Aquasinker. Small and medium-sized lures are the order of the day, white is generally most effective with pale yellow as a change colour, particularly if conditions become bright. A heavy concentration of rainbows and a bright sunny afternoon with a pleasant breeze blowing can also lead to Hot Orange tubes, Whisky Flies, Red Barons and Mickey Finn style lures being effective.

It is usual for something of a lull in the proceedings to set in around tea-time and to last for a couple of hours; the hours from 5 p.m. to 7.30 p.m. are often singularly fruitless, no matter how one fishes. This time should be used for preparing for the main event of mid-season fishing, the evening rise.

Evening fishing from the boats is very unpredictable, and can change from complete hopelessness to frantic activity in the space of ten minutes. It is a true test of one's control and discipline.

Nine times out of ten you have to fish within a couple of feet of the surface to catch fish, the tenth time you need a leadline and a black or white lure, preferably with an inclusion of fluorescence.

With the fish in the topwater, there are two options; lure or small flies. It is not possible to predict which way the fish will go, so it is essential that you have rods set up ready for either alternative.

In both cases, lure and small flies, the main weapon is induction. One does this either by a lot of mechanical flogging or by being more selective and casting very accurately indeed. I use a combination of the two, pulling in quickly and feeling for takes whilst looking around for risers to aim at. Speed is critical, you only have a couple of seconds to lift off and present the fly in front of a customer. The need for speed increases the risk of hooking your partner in the excitement, so take extra care. You also need speed in playing and netting a fish as there is often only a ten minute 'beserk' spell and th¹s comes with practice alone. To cope with the typical variation in fish behaviour during the last hour, one must be prepared to change tactics quickly. Fishing in one style alone will not maximise the catch. Ideally, one needs Floater, Sink-Tip and Wet Cel II rigs all to hand; as soon as takes stop, change over.

Wherever you are fishing, always try and follow ripple, as it is hard to catch them in a flat calm. On windy nights, run your boat down the slicks which concentrate the fish.

There are three types of fly worth bothering with in the last hour: black ones and white ones for under the wave, and a brown Muddler for the surface.

The most useful natural patterns for forward fishing in the evenings tend to be pupae and hatching buzzer and sedge imitations and it is a good idea to rig the cast to present simultaneously a pupa, a hatching pupa and an adult fly. The favoured combination when the sedge are hard on frequently includes Invictas, Soldier Palmers, Seal's fur pupae in a variety of colour combinations with a large Pheasant Tail on the point.

One must never give up hope. One evening in 1979 at Rutland, I rounded off an otherwise blank day with seven fish all over three pounds in the last half hour fishing sedge pupae off the Yachts.

Mid-season fishing, extreme conditions apart, provides the severest test for the boat fisherman's ability to apply radically different methods to cope with frequent and often rapid changes in trout behaviour. It is the period in which the opportunist fisherman, able to cash in very quickly on limited sequencing chances, really enjoys himself.

Backend fishing and the bigger fish

Undoubtedly, most of the really large fish in our waters feed at times and places that inhibit their capture, otherwise they wouldn't grow so large. I feel confident that many more very large fish would be taken if night fishing or motorised deep water trolling with spoons, plugs and dead baits were allowed.

There is no permitted method or tactic which will catch specimen sized trout to the exclusion of all others. Big fish tend to turn up out of the blue except at those specific times when their appearance and probable location can be predicted.

At any time during the season, there are distinct ways of improving one's chances of taking a very large fish; I have picked up the following pointers from fishing Rutland and Grafham over the years.

Grafham yields few exceptionally large brown trout but a large head of middle to heavyweight rainbows. One needs to adopt significantly different tactics when dealing with the two species as it is very rare to find large rainbows and browns in the same place at the same time.

The first five weeks of Grafham's season offer the major chance of taking a specimen fish from a boat. At this time brown trout are active during the daytime and feed at depth. The recommended methods are to troll and leadline over 40 to 60 feet of water, and the area to concentrate on is the north east corner of the reservoir, paying particular attention to fishing along and near the pipeline.

The first week of June has produced some spectacular rainbow catches always in very rough conditions and usually to boats anchored near or alongside the Aeration Tower.

As the season progresses into the summer big fish can be hunted by fishing along the bottom during the early evening, particularly if the day has been bright; and during the last half hour of the day, by fishing 5 to 15 feet deep.

September sees the best chances of taking big fish over the front, particularly in the evenings, the most useful patterns being the Mallard and Claret, Soldier Palmer, Invicta and the Muddler. During the daytime it often pays to put a Daddy on the bob and fish it over the front. The Daddy is one of the few surface flies a really large brownie will move at. On impossibly rough days, dapping can still produce results.

In the late 60's and early 70's Grafham had a considerable amount of disease amongst the perch which resulted in large numbers of fry coming up to the surface and dying. When this happened, it was always signalled by the appearance of terns and seagulls in ones and twos, the birds feeding over the area in which the fry were showing. The tactic was to fish high in the water with white or black lures, over the front or Northampton style depending on the trouts' preference at the time. The Appetizer, floating Baby Doll and Tandem White Muddlers were the great flies with which to fish. The event tended to take place near the S. Buoy shoal and the run into Savages Creek. Perch disease, the great concentrator of fish, has now largely cleared.

The first fortnight of October normally saw a reversion to the early season approach with the leadline and a White Marabou lure. Brownies late on in the season tend to pack into tight shoals to feed very hard but spasmodically through the day. Anchor fishing, particularly in the vicinity of the West Bank and Savages Creek weed beds, often proved the best tactic.

Until September 1982 Grafham has produced the largest reservoir brown trout of recent years from the boats, unfortunately with the captor's subsequent banning for foul fishing a doubt lingers that the fish may have been taken illegally by trolling a spoon.

Anglers seeking real stillwater specimen rainbows are advised to visit Datchet Reservoir and to put up with the noise from nearby Heathrow. Most specimens at Datchet are taken by systematic deep anchor fishing in the vicinity of the draw-off shaft and the 40 foot shelf on the bottom.

The rainbow grown on from a small stockfish, which most reservoir fishermen would recognise as the real British record was taken at Datchet some years ago. It weighed around 14 lb., and never received the recognition it deserved, largely due to the current practice of dumping old, flabby, overweight, brood fish into waters incapable of producing anything naturally other than stunted roach.

In contrast to Grafham, Rutland produces very few large rainbows. I suspect this is due to a combination of disease, lack of adequate spawn-shedding facilities, and close-season poaching in the feeder streams which together lead to the survival of very few rainbows into their second season in the reservoir. At Grafham, 16 per cent of my total catch were overwintered rainbows; at Rutland the figure was 1.5 per cent for the combined seasons 1978–81. One hopes that conditions will change and the situation will improve. Fortunately, Rutland Water is the main producer of large brown trout in the U.K. and it is only a matter of time before it produces the reservoir record, probably during the 1983–4 seasons, provided it is spared a major tapeworm infestation. Rutland's importance is likely to decline unless there is a radical increase in the numbers of brown trout to be stocked.

Certain similarities exist between Rutland and Grafham in behaviour patterns of big fish; the times and basic situations of activity are almost identical. Indeed only the locations of the activity in terms of depth differ to any marked degree.

The first six weeks of Rutland's season provide the initial opportunity. This is best undertaken by drift leadlining over water 15–50 feet deep which can be found anywhere from midway down the Arms right into the shallows in the rough cold winds that can be expected during May. Fishing for the better brownies is more profitable after a mild winter than a hard one; a hard winter implies a lack of feeding and this prevents the fish returning to condition.

Such larger rainbows as there are shoal up in early June and move into relatively shallow water at the ends of both Arms, particularly into the Gwash shallows to the south west of Lax Hill. There is maybe a fortnight of spasmodic daytime feeding activity before the packs disperse. During this period the packs remain fairly stationary and the best approach is to fish quietly at anchor. The fishing can be fascinating and often very challenging.

During high summer conditions big brown trout can be taken on almost any bright day when there is just enough wind to ripple the surface. The killing technique involves longfall fishing with either small or large White or Pale Yellow tube flies over depths between 25 and 40 feet. The best times are from around 4 p.m. in the afternoon until dark. Long pulsed retrieves, coming up from deep on a very flat retrieve path, are required. It is rare for large numbers of fish to be taken at this time of year due to the apparent reluctance of the bigger fish to take a proper hold of the fly. Much frustration will be experienced at the frequent stop, tap, pull-back and thickwater takes, almost all of which will prove unhittable. On one memorable day in 1978, I had 42 of these takes before eventually connecting with a 4 lb. fish at 7.30 p.m. in the evening; it was a grey day, the very worst overhead conditions for taking better fish by these means.

Heavy wind conditions in mid and late summer, frequently presage the appearance of a few very large fish high in the water. Forward fishing with sedge patterns is probably the best way of taking such fish although dapping should never be discounted, especially after mid August.

During July and August very large fish have become active in the last few seasons, but always at great depth. Continuous leadline and varied retrieve hold-on fishing has proved the only way of catching such fish, which usually lie about 40 feet down in 50 to 110 feet of water. Large white, black, fluorescent limegreen or flectolite lures up to 5 inches long, are the killing patterns.

In the middle of the day during September, Rutland's brown trout are usually to be found high in the water. There is no better way of tackling them than by fishing over the front, either with sedge representations or with small Black Lures or Tadpoles. Deeper lying fish respond well to large Black and Silver lures throughout the month.

As September progresses into October, cock brownies gather in packs, usually revealed by the behaviour of 'priming' in which odd large fish will jump well clear of the water. This jumping occurs at random throughout the day, but intensifies in the early morning from daybreak up until around 10 a.m. and in the last hours of light. If one is fortunate enough to be able to drift through one of these packs early or late in the day, and if conditions are calm enough to permit long and accurate casting, it is often possible to have half an hour of real sport. The technique is to side-swipe at leapers and through the area of general activity using large all-Black Marabou or Hairwing lures in tandem or triple L/S 6's. The angle of the fly to the light is particularly critical; it isn't simply a matter of turfing the fly out at right angles to the boat and pulling away; often the fish will only take the fly coming pretty nearly straight back down the wind. One has to experiment by casting at different angles.

This method can produce savage takes which almost immediately come unstuck, to the absolute amazement of the fisherman. This, I suspect, is caused by the fact that the old cock brownies are not going after the lure to eat it, merely to bite it very hard to warn it not to come back. A trout determined to eat a lure will attempt to swallow it into the back of the throat; a biter will grab the lure with the front of its jaws where its teeth are. The only way of having a fair chance of hooking a few of these old cock fish is to make certain that one's lure hooks are of the very best quality, tough, wide-gaped, short-pointed (to drive into gristle and hold) and as sharp as razors.

Rough water disperses these packs which usually assemble off the Three Trees on the east bank, in the centre of the North Arm about 200 yards offshore from the Hedge Ends on the A606 bank and along the Causeway in the South Arm. When dispersed from the surface layers by the wind, it is occasionally possible to take these fish by fishing deep through the area on the lead or the Aquasinker.

The great majority of the hen fish, first season fish, and only a few cock fish pack into the east bank between Normanton Church and the Dam. Generally, during the daytime, these fish will hold on a line between 50 and 90 yards offshore.

With the onset of the first frosts the fish will nose-dive towards the bottom and are only really takeable with the leadline fished either at anchor or on the drift when the wind permits. White lures are almost mandatory, particularly the White Christmas Tree. Feeding is patchy with one day producing nothing and the next a spectacular double limit. Calm weather often sees the fish lift up in the water where they can be dealt with by using a Super Aquasink shooting head fished in pitch and pay style.

There are, late in the season, a very few large rainbows about in the South Arm, mixed in with a number of first year fish. These fish are only takeable at anchor, with the lead, over 25 plus feet of water. Orange throated white lures and Dog Nobblers have been generally the most successful patterns in recent seasons.

Some seasons are 'early' and some are late. Backend fishing for bigger browns in a late season is worthwhile, the fish will still be in good condition, the hens are not yet heavily gravid nor the cocks yet dark and slimy. Fish for browns in the backend of an early season and the catch is not worth having.

Larger numbers of very heavy fish are taken from the bank than from the boats. This is because bank fishing usually starts earlier in the day (sometimes the night before) and finishes later in the day. Big fish do most of their feeding during the hours of darkness; alas, we boat fishermen are not allowed out at night.

The 1982 season at Rutland saw an increase in the practice of fishing at anchor in close proximity to cages in which stockfish were being reared. Beneath the cages dwelt numbers of large old trout which had taken to living on surplus pellets dropping through the mesh of the cages above. As a result, many of these fish were caught; indeed, Fred Wagstaffe took three over 9 lb. in one day. I have no liking of this tactic – but it *is* highly effective.

Stockies

It is possible to deliberately catch stockfish and this should be done
if there is nothing else feeding. Stockfishing can be amusing and
frustrating, stockfish tend to be very pawky indeed when taking a
fly; I can recall a two-hour spell fishing a line deep and having a take
on virtually every cast, on some casts rather more than one. I
actually boated three fish. Most missed takes are due to stockfish.

When facing an abundance of stockfish, be strictly practical in
your attitude to taking them. Rainbows do not survive long in
Britain, so a stock rainbow should be killed immediately; brownies
grow on so put them back unless they are bleeding. Never shake a
fish off the hook, wet your hands, take them gently from the net, use
artery forceps to get the hook out quickly with as little damage
as possible, then return them. A fish shaken off may be worse
damaged than you think. If the rules permit it, return little fish.
Where, however, you are forced to take runty little devils, console
yourself with the thought that you are only abetting a crime; the real
'criminals' are the villains who put them in undersized.

Stock rainbows have the following characteristics: they hold
together in a shoal, they usually dive for the bottom within two days
of introduction and they tend to move off from the mobbing spot in
an upwind direction; almost invariably they will surface and feed
crazily in the last hour of light.

Stock brownies hold deep right from the start of the season up
until July. They follow well-known routes at Rutland and can be
chased from the Dam right round to the Yacht Club before they
disperse at the end of June. Depending upon the water, there will be
mobbing points for early in the season and dispersal routes usually
following the line of the shore from which the prevailing wind
blows.

Quite often it pays to seek out packs of stockfish and then to fish
deliberately underneath them with large lures. This can often result
in catching large brown trout and pike, which in the large sizes are
not to be despised as sport fish. The best brace of fly-caught pike
taken from Rutland in 1979 jointly weighed 21¼ lb. Jim Clements
had one of 11½ lb., mine weighed 9¾ lb. His took a size 6
Appetizer, mine a size 8 Missionary, they came on consecutive
casts; nearby were stockfish! A sensible tactic is to go and catch a few
stockies before you start serious fishing. Even more sensible is to

remember where they were in the morning if you need to complete your limit at night.

The best way of avoiding stockfish is to move away to another area altogether. This may cost you your limit: you will, however, end the day feeling very virtuous indeed!

Boils lore

Many of our reservoirs, particularly the modern flatland ones, possess one or both of two features that can radically affect the fishing in their immediate vicinity: aerators or pumped storage pipelines. Both of these features achieve their effect by moving columns of water vertically in the reservoir, either by air-lift in the case of aerators or by an inflow current. The effects of both these features are similar, both are due to the current they induce. These currents are always heavily aerated and are also, on occasion, full of food swept up from the bottom by the upwelling column of water. The two types of boil should be approached differently as they are somewhat different in cause and also tend to operate at different times of the year.

Aerators are turned on during calm days in the height of summer to ensure the quality of water to be drawn off for public consumption. At these times the rest of the reservoir is less oxygenated than normal, and the fish more inclined to sulk. During the daytime in high summer, it often pays to fish deep around and through water that has been oxygenated by aerator boils. In the flat calms of June and July, rainbows and browns both will hold deep for most of the day, rising to the top in the evening from 7.30 p.m. onwards and staying on the top through the night and into the early morning. On odd occasions such fish will stay high in the water until as late as 11 a.m.

At the first sight of a boil, it might seem obvious that what one should do is to anchor the boat and fish right into the disturbed water upwelling from below. This is normally the wrong thing to do as fish tend to hang just off the boil in the downwind tail slicks, taking advantage both of the aerated water being drifted down to them by the wind and the food that the water contains, usually shrimp, snail and water hoglice.

The way to fish a boil is to start from 150 yards upwind and then to drift down one side. Quite frequently, in an evening, the fish will

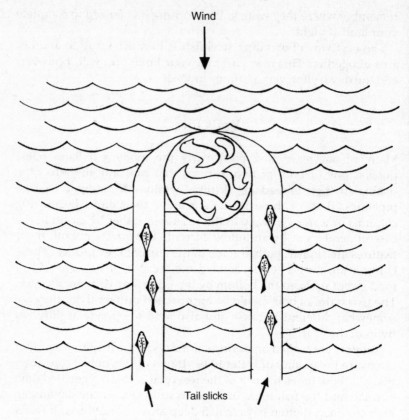

Fig. 28   Boil effects: fish running in tail slicks

move upwind of a boil and stay well clear of the aerated water.

On some waters there are a number of different aerators and it is usual for several to be working simultaneously. Strangely, fish will tend to concentrate around one particular boil especially in the evening, so fish round all the boils quickly, find out which one the fish are on and then stay there until time to go. The best evening tactics are sideswiping lures, either White Marabou Tandems, the White Tube or a Black Marabou Tandem in the last half hour. Very occasionally, fish working on the boils will not take the lure. Appropriate flies for forward fishing are the Soldier Palmer, Cinnamon and Gold and Sienna Sedge or Hare's Ear.

Pumping boils tend to be fairly unproductive in the evening, but they usually do hold fish during the morning and afternoon. Often pumped water is a different colour from the reservoir and when this happens the area should be fished just like a stain line, by casting into the coloured water and then fishing into the clear. Pumping tends to take place early and late in the season and depends upon the supply rivers being full of water. Early in the season, even the rising fish around the boils, being somewhat foolish will take hold of a lure. Later on in the season quite a high proportion of the food in the vicinity of pumped water will be beaten-up fry, dragged into the current and forced up to the surface. A large Appetizer fished high or low will usually suffice.

Late on in the season it can pay to anchor on the boil and fish deep with a leadline and a very large White Lure. Anchoring on a boil is by no means easy as the upwelling water tends to push the boat off station. It is often necessary to use two or three anchors set round the boil to get the boat positioned exactly where you want it. We used to fish at Grafham this way, fish were fairly hard to come by but spectacular when they did; four fish a day between two of us was the average, either big brownies or big pike!

8 *Weather*
Situations

Rain

Rain is usually associated with the passing of a frontal system. Boat-fishing is not improved by rain; the noise or maybe the barometric pressure fluctuations unsettle the fish.

Often, the fish themselves will signal the onset of rain by feeding very hard immediately before it starts; particularly if the onset is accompanied by half an hour or so of rising wind. It is important to fish hard before the rain arrives, for when it does the fish are likely to go suddenly off the boil.

There are two varieties of frontal rain: warm front rain and cold front rain. With a warm front, there is usually increased activity on the part of the flylife in the water. Hatches are very likely within an hour of the rain starting and usually bring the fish high up into the water where they may be expected to take again after the initial lull. Tactical approaches to warm frontal rain are the obvious ones of fishing over the front with the floater or sink tip, or using Northampton style tactics for fishing high, coupled with small lures.

Occasionally, in continuous warm rain and low wind conditions, trolling will outfish all other methods, particularly shallow trolling with the sink tip and Wet Cel II shooting heads. Again, small lures are the order of the day with the Appetizer and small White tubes being of particular value.

Cold front rain is much less pleasant and usually implies that the fish will dive deep and stay there.

I am of the opinion that the grey overhead conditions that accompany rain are unusually helpful to the trout's powers of vision. I am also certain that they can see far better in poor light than in brilliant sunlight and as a result it is exceptionally difficult to take fish by fishing very deep during rain in midseason. Midwater fishing with medium-sized lures is a much better prospect. Cold front rain usually means that the Super Aquasinker shooting head, the L/S 6 lure and the long leader fished Northampton style becomes the order of the day; the lure has to be down to between 10 and 20 feet, no shallower, no deeper.

Rain can be insidious. In mid-season it often starts very gently and the engrossed fisherman may not notice how wet he and his tackle are getting before the damage has been done and the body and the flyboxes are sodden.

If rain is approaching, an attempt should be made to organise the tackle to minimise the effects and this is best undertaken with a couple of plastic bin liners. Every spare item that does not need to be exposed should be packed away, including the lunch (waterlogged sandwiches are revolting), all unnecessary flyboxes and tackle bags, which always let the water in. In packing gear into bin liners remember that the rain will seek out every entry; instead of leaving the open end pointing towards the heavens and acting as a funnel, tuck it under. If flyboxes do get waterlogged, the rusting and discolouration of flies can be minimised by using Ethafoam to line the boxes; that and opening the boxes up and putting them on top of the central heating boiler as soon as you get home. The recent development of glassfibre coarse fishing tackle boxes has minimised my problems in this respect. They can hold an enormous amount of equipment and are watertight. Mine was manufactured by Messrs Shakespeare.

Being short-sighted and bespectacled, I have problems in seeing when it rains. A baseball cap or some other form of headgear with a long peak or a wide brim is the answer. I find the baseball cap style best as one can wear them with the hood of a jacket up.

Waterproof clothing should always be donned before the rain starts; failing that, at the very first drop. This delays the annoying dampness. I say delays, because in sustained rain nothing except, possibly, having oneself vulcanised will prevent one from getting wet. If your gear is good enough to stop the rain getting in, it will be good enough to prevent the perspiration getting out. To further delay the process, fish standing up as sitting down greatly increases the wetness penetrating the nether regions. One invaluable tip is to ensure that the overtrousers are worn outside the boots.

With cold front rain, accompanied by wind, exposure effects can ruin the day. The particular point of attack is the hands; the wind chill factor is greatly multiplied over wet hands and swelling and rheumatism of the fingers prevent effective fishing. It is generally a waste of time to fish in gloves, unless one is trolling when sensitivity of response is irrelevant. One method of reducing wind chill effects without the use of gloves is to vaseline the hands before setting out.

Cigarettes, pipes, matches, lighters, tobacco, paper money and fishing permits should be kept somewhere warm and dry. I keep mine three layers in from the waterproofs; this is usually sufficient. A more sensible idea would be to put everything, bar the cigarettes and the matches (always carry spares of these particular items) inside the glass fibre tackle box; alas, I rarely remember to do this until it is too late.

Big winds

Fishing in big winds is usually productive, it can also be dangerous. Before outlining tactics, some pointers on safety are required. Relatively little danger exists whilst a boat is drifting downwind, even through massive waves. The real trouble starts when an attempt is made to turn the boat and go back up wind. Driving into a heavy wave takes patience, an ability to think clearly when afraid and considerable boatmanship. To stand any chance of getting upwind in dangerous waves, the bows must be held down to prevent the wind getting under and broaching the boat. The passenger must move to the bows and lie down securely before setting off. The boat should be driven as slowly as possible consistent with keeping steerage way; full throttle in heavy seas will put extreme stresses on the boat and occupants and can lead to fractures of both. It is often safer to run across and downwind to calmer water even if this means taking the long way round.

If the worst happens and the boat overturns, attempt to stay with the floating hulk until you are either rescued or blown ashore. Everyone should possess a lifejacket and should wear it when conditions are appropriate; the £25 or so involved is much cheaper than the cost of a burial.

Have no fears about being blown onto a leeshore, you might be bruised by the experience but you are unlikely to be drowned unless knocked unconscious against a stone dam; reduce the risk of this by swimming in feet first instead of head first.

If a sudden savage wind blows up, the only real option is to shelter under the windward shore, particularly in the lee of happily placed hillsides or forestry plantations. In such spots, nose down anchoring is the order of the day; this reduces the likelihood of the anchor dragging. It is very difficult to hold a square-on anchored boat in a rough wind and the exercise of having to go back and reanchor from time to time is one of the best ways of disturbing fish. At the limit, put the anchors onshore or tie the rope to a convenient tree. I once fished in a wind at Grafham so strong (gusting to 60 m.p.h.) that the boat dragged two heavy anchors thrown well up onshore. We caught nothing that day.

Most fisheries will not allow boatfishing in windspeeds greater than Beaufort Force 6; if you go out in a boat and conditions deteriorate past this point (usually identifiable by the start of spin-drift and the feeling that you are being hit in the face by hail stones rather than spray when motoring upwind) either anchor in a sheltered spot or get off the water altogether.

Tactics

Safety dictates that it is unwise to fish most leeshore water and this places the first major limitation on the tactics open in a high wind. The other major limitations are the speed of the boat when drifting and the difficulty of handling tackle, particularly in casting.

Anchoring

When anchored in a really bad wind, restrict the distances cast. The accompanying ripple renders the boat less visible to fish in any event, and they are likely to be less put off by the noise of heavy lines landing.

Occasionally, pressure vacuums form on the downwind side of the fisherman. This phenomenon causes the backing to lift up from the deck and tangle itself most fearsomely. One way of overcoming this problem is for each fisherman to wear a large line tray to keep the backing in some semblance of order.

One should attempt to work through as many of the tactical variations outlined in the chapter on anchor fishing as are possible in the conditions. It is very easy to become disheartened by the hopelessness of it all, and to start to flog away mechanically. If this happens, expect to catch nothing whatsoever. Every attempt must be made to keep the spirits high and the interest engaged, keep moving the boat about looking for productive spots and above all keep working. If all else fails, have a kip and get ready to fish flat out if the wind slackens off in the evening.

When drifting is safe the major fishing problem is to accommodate the speed of the boat. Obviously when the wind blows hard the boat will run fast. This can be advantageous in the middle of the season, June, July, August and September, when rainbows often become enervated by the rough conditions and can be taken out of the top of the wave by one of the variations of hold-on fishing with slower sinking lines. However, at other times it is usually necessary to slow the boat either by use of drogues or by steering to spill the wind. This is because to fish deep it is essential to give the line time to settle and with a fast running boat this is difficult to accomplish with shooting heads. Use of the continuous leadline becomes mandatory when one wishes to fish very deep and run the boat quickly at the same time.

In all Northampton styles the man at the helm always has the problem of casting with the wind coming directly over his wrong shoulder. As the wind increases casting becomes difficult and then downright dangerous. The helmsman has three options:

(1) Turn the boat until the wind is coming straight into the left hand quarter and cast forward directly into the wind.
(2) Turn the boat into the right hand quarter and cast backhanded.
(3) Fishing without casting.

Apart from hold-on fishing, the commonest useful retrieve method is the semi-duplication of the pitch and pay technique: allowing all the backing to stream out and pulling back in as soon as everything goes tight.

The retrieve speed has to be varied to suit the inclination of the fish and this can vary widely from day to day and even from hour to hour. (This method can also be used by beginners and disabled anglers as routine, if they are unable to cast. It will work well on its day under normal weather conditions.) With a fast drift, it is impossible to produce a slow retrieve with this method and others have to be used.

The pumped retrieve is the next option, when the backing has streamed out the fisherman pumps in and out keeping a fixed amount of backing out behind the shooting head. This has the effect of producing a spurt-pause retrieve at one depth.

It is possible, by gauging the speeds at which one pumps the retrieve, to vary the action on the fly considerably:

Spurt/Halt   Backhand pull fast, push at the same speed as the boat runs.

Spurt/Slow Travel   Backhand pull fast, push at slower speed than the boat is running.

On the day, the fish will either want the fly coming to a halt or merely slowing its pace.

Occasionally one will be fishing too fast even with pumping, and then the payback technique has to be used. Payback fishing allows the fly to be worked through a range of depths and thus enables one to run a search pattern on the days when fish are varying their feeding depth.

The basic fishing method is to pay the line steadily back under control and against the pressure generated by the running speed of the boat. Again, as with pump retrieving, great care must be taken to vary the pace and the amount of the payback.

Very often, running at extreme speed, payback fishing works particularly well with the leadcored shooting head followed by as little as 20 yards of monofilament. This is because of the lift effect of big waves. Often, even the Super Aquasink shooting head is too light to cut downwards through heavy surface turbulence.

Flies suitable for these styles of fishing usually tend to be fairly substantial; the rule is the rougher the water, the larger the fly that can be used. As a standard first approach in all conditions, I would advocate the use of plain white tandem lures or tube flies, equally useful is the White Christmas Tree in tandem 8's or 6's size.

If conditions are bright and fish are lying deep, the use of large lures incorporating strips of georeflective plastic is often effective. Different light conditions determine which flash is best: copper, silver or gold – experimentation is necessary.

As in all forms of deep fishing, it is essential to find the precise depth of the feeding fish. This is particularly difficult in heavy waves if the fish are running high in the water. In such a situation, the business of getting down to the correct depth is complicated by the turbulence which retards the sinking rates of virtually all lines except true leadcored ones. A useful device for taking high feeding fish just below the mean trough level is to use a doubled line consisting of two full forward tapers spliced together at the end of the shooting line. At the limit fish lying 15 feet deep can be taken either on a doubled Forward Taper Super Aquasinker or by fishing short with a leadcored head with 25 yards of monofil paid out.

If it is safe to do so fish down onto leeshores or past outlying promontories. Inevitably, the leeshore water will be heavily churned up and muddy; fish the three hundred yards upwind and down into the start of the stain. Fish will rarely be taken in thickly muddied water but can usually be relied upon to be lying just off the mirk. Shallow shoaling water often gets knocked up forming muddy lines in the water and it often pays to fish by running down the clear water just off such a mudslick casting into the mirk and retrieving the flies out into cleaner water. If casting is not feasible, hold-on and snake the boat downwind on the rudder, steering in and out of the stain to produce a similar effect.

Forward fishing in very rough conditions is rather a waste of time unless the boat can be slowed down sufficiently to permit a proper retrieve. Heavy droguing is required to fish the boat square on, and often a far better alternative is to fish the boat angled across the wind using one or two large drogues over the stern quarter.

To some extent, the speed of the boat will be governed by the pressure of the waves. For this reason it often means that fishing forward is better suited to fishing off the windward shore, rather than onto a leeshore.

A big wind in midseason is usually associated with heavy chironomid hatches, in addition to the multiplicity of insects blown onto the water from the land. If one can find some sheltered upwind water, especially very shallow water, then conditions of heavy wind are particularly appropriate for fishing teams of buzzer imitations, including winged and hackled variants to represent drowned hatching adults.

Later on in the season, dapping with the daddy, particularly if used in conjunction with a heavy point fly acting as a sheet anchor can prove very effective.

In October, after the onset of the first frosts, it is unlikely that fish will feed high in the water again. Fishing in a heavy wind at this time of year usually requires use of continuous leadline to get the fly down the 20 feet plus to the feeding fish. At such times it is not uncommon to find odd large brown trout active higher in the water until around 11 a.m. These higher running fish can usually be taken with a Super Aquasink shooting head. After around 11 a.m. the fish seem to leave the turbulent upper water and head for the quieter deeps and it then requires a leadcored shooting head or a long leadline to get back onto terms with them.

One worthwhile experiment in these circumstances is to attach (by the loop through loop method) three to five yards of AFTM 9 level floating line to the end of the continuous leadline. This rig can be fished with the tip of the leadline bouncing across the bottom, the floater will hold the fly (which should be either lightweight or better, positively buoyant) just above the bottom. This technique works best in the latter part of the year when weed growth has begun to die back; it is rather ineffective applied over shallow water in mid-season.

In October and in high winds the frequency of takes drops to as few as 5 to 10 actual takes in the day. Unless one has both highly trained reflexes and an ability to concentrate hard over long periods fishing heavy winds late on in the season can be a singularly fruitless occupation.

Flat calms

Of all the weather situations, the very worst for boatfishing is a glass flat. As the wind dies the stimuli that make fish run die as well and the absence of ripple rules out drift fishing. Every sound and every motion warns any fish within range of the angler's presence.

Odging

The standby tactic for fishing in flat calms is called odging and the procedure runs thus:

(1) Both fishermen cast out and pay backing into the water.
(2) One oar is picked up and used to paddle the boat gently away in nose down style. The boat is paddled just enough to come to a stop at the limit of the loose backing.
(3) The retrieve cycle commences as the boat stops.

This tactic is laborious, sweaty and a damned nuisance to keep up for hours at a stretch. It will, however, keep you fishing with a chance of a fish. It is usually more profitable to fish deep, getting the flies close to the bottom as, on occasion, a few fish will be mooching about picking off small pupae ascending from the weed.

The quality of light at depth in a flat calm often means that the fish can see terminal tackle a lot more clearly than with a good ripple overhead. It is well worth using smaller lures than normal and both extending the leader and lightening it. Size 8 L/S lures are appropriate with the leader altered from 16 feet of 13 lb. BS to 22 feet of 8 lb. BS.

One device worth trying is to fish on a line running away from the sun, the light direction is better for deception. Backdragging deep nymph rigs at very slow speeds can also be profitable. This technique relies on the fact that there will often be a fractional movement of the boat; the surface layer usually has some semblance of movement in it left over from the last wind.

Using floating line and a leader 24 to 30 feet long and rigging with heavy flies i.e. a 7780c Pheasant Tail, a leaded shrimp or Stick Fly, cast over the back and sit very quietly as it settles. Fish either by going to sleep or by pulling in about 5 yards at a foot a time. When pulling, watch the curve of the line between rod tip and water, if it doesn't fall back after a pull, strike immediately. A combination of backdrag and odge can be worked by presenting the nymphs on a sinking tip.

Jigging, a technique heavily used in North America but almost unknown in the United Kingdom, can be put to good use but only if the boat is kept absolutely silent. Using a continuous leadline, a short leader and a heavily leaded fly, lower the tackle straight down into the water and feel for the bottom with the jig. Fish by raising and lowering the rod point no more than six inches and watch out for sharp takes. Jigging is rather better applied over a clean bottom; over weed it is usually necessary to use either a keel hooked jig, which ensures that most of the takes will be missed due to the dreadful hooking performance of keel hooks; or an offset jig that will fish the fly on its back with the hook point uppermost.

Trolling is rarely particularly productive in a glass flat unless you can find a heavy concentration of stock rainbows. On occasions, though, at Grafham and particularly in bright sunlight odd big rainbows can be caught trolling in the middle with 40 yards of continuous leadline out and very large Black or White lures attached.

The thermocline, vastly over emphasised in its importance to still-water fishermen over the last 20 years, only comes into effect in high summer after a long period of still weather. 1975 and 1976 were the last years in which the thermocline had any real effect on the fishing. At those times, the thermocline occurred between 15 and 21 feet deep at Grafham. To take fish one had merely to ensure that one fished close to the bottom in water around that depth. Odging, the leadcored shooting head and tandem Black Marabou lures proved the answer to the problems posed by those years. The area to concentrate on was the shoaling water around S. Buoy. Hot still weather with attendant high water temperatures eventually sickens fish; all the rainbows that we took during that period were extensively leech marked on their bellies, clear evidence that they had been lying on the bottom for a long time, most unusual behaviour for rainbow trout.

Very occasionally, it will pay to fish high in the water in a flat calm; only, however, when fish can actually be seen rising. The technique is to stay seated in the boat and to try to pitch your flies just in front of a riser; as there is no wind and, therefore, nothing to make the fish move in a specific direction, it is essential to study the rise to determine which way the fish is going; rises ·are generally egg-shaped, drop your flies a couple of yards in front of the blunt end, let them settle and pull.

An alternative to this method is to use fairly light and slow settling flies and a little patience. Throw out and wait, when a fish rises within a couple of yards of the end of the line, start pulling. Takes to this method are usually ferocious, so watch for line burns. Arthur Cove advocates the use of a team consisting of a size 14 Black buzzer, a size 14 Green buzzer and a size 12 Invicta on the point; he is rarely wrong (occasionally a small Grenadier will do the trick, on the point).

One must pay attention to what is happening to the weather. It is rare for a flat calm to persist throughout the day and, as the calm breaks, there will often be small patches of ripple struck up by changes in the air pattern. As a ripple begins, run the boat for it and fish down it until it peters out, then look around for the next patch of ripple. It is usually possible to take fish high in the water in a ripple patch and it always pays to have a go when the chance is offered; it may be the only one of the day.

Evening flat calms are rather easier to catch fish in than daytime flat calms. Normally it is profitable to fish with a team of sedge or buzzer pupae, depending upon the time of the season and the insect in the air. From time to time, fish can be taken with a muddler either

by throwing at risers and stripping through to make a wake or by
greasing it solid and using it as a dry fly. All evenings are different
and one has to be prepared to change rapidly from one tactic to
another.

9 Managing the fishing day

A day's fishing does not commence with the first cast; indeed, the fishing itself should be the tip of the iceberg, the time when the planning, the tactics, theories and strategies are put into practice. There is no way that a disorganised approach will yield consistent success and thorough preparation makes up the bulk of the iceberg.

Weather forecasting

For me, the fishing day begins about three days before I actually go when I start paying attention to the weather forecasts. The forecast for the day itself rarely predicts with accuracy such seeming inessentials as windspeed, arrival of frontal systems, overhead light conditions, whether it will rain or not etc., etc. To overcome this one has to do the job oneself working from the pattern of weather on the previous days and the published pressure system maps in the papers. I also listen to the coastal forecasts and have even been known to place some reliance on the BBC Sunday Farming Forecast for the week. In any event, no officially produced short term forecast is given in sufficient accuracy for fishermen. Another problem is that large sheets of water significantly affect the micro-climate in their immediate vicinity, each water in its own particular way. The only answer is to keep on fishing a water and eventually do your own short term weather forecasting on the basis of your local knowledge combined with published forecasts.

Very occasionally, when I suspect that something nasty may occur, I will ring up the nearest aerodrome and ask them for a short term forecast on the morning before fishing. In my time, I have fished in a waterspout at Grafham and experienced other horrors, including the very worst possible, a thunderstorm. The only weather-induced fatality on fisheries known to me locally occurred some years ago at Draycote Reservoir in an electrical storm; the unfortunate fisherman collected several megajoules of energy in a very short time. His partner was more fortunate – he lived. If caught in a thunderstorm, don't wave a carbon fibre rod about, graphite is as conductive as steel, some 10 times more conductive than water and a great deal more conductive than a fibreglass rod. This suggests that it should be relatively safe to fish on with a fibreglass rod. In practice, however, you, your rod, your clothing and your boots are likely to be wet through, raising your conductivity to the general level of your surroundings; after that, its down to random chance. My advice is to get ashore and lie down in a ditch!

Weather is a critical factor in determining success; as it changes it will rule out certain tactical options and open others up. Go prepared with as much advance information as possible.

Pooling information

If you have reliable information about the way the water has fished in the days immediately preceding your visit, a lot of the uncertainty may be taken out of your planning. I say 'may' because the pattern of events changes daily; it often makes more sense to rely upon your judgement of what is likely to happen than to go blithely forth and exactly duplicate the tactics that your best friend took his limit with the day before. Different fish populations feed at different times; one day it will be two-years-in fish; the next stock rainbows; the next one-year-in browns. Trout, being cold-blooded, do not need three square meals a day. To maintain weight they need one square meal every three days; to put on weight, two square meals every three days. When a population has fed hard one day, it is more than likely to be somewhat comatose the next.

Also, your sources will not have been able to make a thorough assessment. For example, one can fish hard, long and successfully in the Rutland's North Arm for the day; the South Arm and the Trolling Area may have fished better and will certainly have fished very differently. Rely solely upon your informants and you may be missing out on the beanfeast of the century a mile from where they were successful the day before.

Nevertheless, it helps if one can develop a network of friends who fish the water on different days of the week. Jim Clements and I work closely with a circle of four other Rutlanders. During the week we ring each other up and pool information. We all do well and this may have something to do with it; six heads are certainly better than one.

Anybody can make friends by being honest and open with information. It pays dividends in terms of fish taken and there is a great deal of scope for mateyness when afloat. Be pleased if you put people onto fish, one day they will help you out of a certain blank.

Every fisherman should maintain a record system of some kind. Ideally this should not be kept in the form of a fishing diary as previously noted. A simple card system is much easier to refer to; all that is required as essential homework is a quick flick through the cards for a fortnight on either side of the next fishing date. This should alert one to all the possibilities that have worked in the past. The older I become the easier it is to forget tactical possiblities.

Loading

There is no excuse for forgetting essential items of tackle but it still happens to me with regrettable frequency. Everyone should have a checklist of equipment and a simple routine to follow. I pack the car early on the evening before. Although not a teetotaller, I take my fishing sufficiently seriously to ensure that I do not drink heavily before a fishing trip. As a result I have never arrived at the water with a crashing hangover. Some of my partners have and wasted whole days as a result.

On the way to the water my partner and I tend to pass the time in mulling over the prospects and working out where to go during the day and in what order. By the time we arrive, we invariably have a plan of campaign worked out.

We load the boat in line with the style that we are going to commence fishing in. We never assemble all our rods before we get into the boat. Most of the time, you fish through the day with only one rod and line so there is little point in each partner setting up three or four rods. A lot of rods leads to massive tangles and a fair chance of a breakage during the day.

If you have planned to fish close to the boat moorings then, by all means, set up the one rod that you intend to use initially, but no more. If you are going to travel for any length of time, don't set rods up until you are under way, keep clutter in the boat to a minimum.

Matching tactics to strengths

On many days in the season there is no one right way to fish. Different populations of trout will be on the fin and the larger the water the greater the dispersal of those populations. Typically, different feeding behaviours will be apparent in different areas of the water.

In practice, this leads one into having to make very difficult decisions as to how to fish and where. Take, for example, a warm July day at Rutland when simultaneously you can expect to take rainbows out of the top by shortlining with small flies in the South Arm, brownies out of deep water in the North Arm with a Super Aquasink shooting head and a small White tube and better rainbows by fishing deep nymph at anchor in the Gwash shallows. What should one do? The answer is not easy, if all methods will work equally well. However, more often than not the potential of each method will vary. In racing terms it may be 2 to 1 on with short-lining, even money at anchor and 3 to 1 against by going with the Super Aquasink.

Each fisherman has his foibles and fortés in terms of ability in applying various methods and it may well pay to fish highly effectively at odds of 3 to 1 against than very ineffectively at much better odds.

One certain conclusion emerges from the problem; the greater the angler's ability to handle the different methods, the wider the options become and the better the chance of fishing successfully to the highest quality fish moving on the day.

You should select the method for the day which is likely to be the most rewarding to you. Your objectives are as legitimate as anybody else's, be they numbers, gross weight, big fish, improving skills, the pursuit of difficult fish by intrinsically difficult methods or whatever.

And so what happens in practice? You set off and fish away until you start hitting fish. Earlier comments on deep fishing with reference to sequencing are equally applicable to all styles and tactics. One must be able to exactly duplicate the sequence of events that led to the capture of the first fish. Fishing is not like golf, a game of near mishits, it is 100 per cent duplication or nothing. All the factors must be duplicated exactly and at speed before conditions alter or one drifts through the fish. To do this effectively, you must have a framework of reference to go back to.

One of the hardest things is to remember exactly what one did on the cast that took a fish, after playing it out and the resulting commotion of boating, priesting and admiring it. The easiest way is to recap as soon as the hook goes in. If that method does not work for you, then recourse must be made to a systematic approach to each cast.

In Northampton style fishing and anchor fishing the concept of microvariation is central to the business of taking fish. It is an essential part of both styles to fish each cast differently: a different angle, a different payout, a different swing, a different stopwatch timing; there are many variations of depth, retrieve, angle and speeds to be worked through. Less well-known is the need in forward fishing to vary presentation; angles to the boat are critical and often the practical difference of casting 10° one way or the other is all that is required to make the difference between a lot of fish and no fish at all. Normally, in topwater fishing the angle of light, relative to the flies is a factor of crucial significance; a fly that appears lifeless at one angle will be taken without hesitation when presented at another. What one has to do is to arrange to put each cast out at a slightly different angle in rotation and to work the presentation cycle thus generated repetitively until one encounters a fish. Casting forwards at random materially reduces effectiveness.

Once the killing microvariation has been found the next problem is to overcome the sequence that finishes before the boat has been filled. There are a number of reasons for this, the major ones being scaring out of the area, change in depth, change in feeding pattern, and cessation of feeding. All dictate that to re-establish contact with the fish, you must change your approach: the area, the fishing depth, the lure or fly, the action of the flies. The other alternative is to flog away until the fish decide to take again; this is not recommended as it constitutes behaviour akin to a stopped clock. A stopped clock is right twice, for a very short time, in twenty-four hours.

It is occasionally quite difficult to distinguish between when the fish have been truly lost and when the statistical possibility of just not showing the fly to a fish has occurred. Two short, blank drifts through an area that was previously active should be all the indication that you need!

The last noteworthy point is the phenomenon of the fishing instinct. Mechanical following of set search patterns will catch an awful lot of fish, but the development of an instinctive feel will catch even more if properly applied. Instinct develops with experience. Increasingly over the years, the small voice of instinct tells me to do something and I do it, and catch a fish immediately. Sometimes the instinct is useful in that it operates negatively telling me that a drift or a method just feels wrong. The 'on the spot' integration of all the factors that are required to catch a fish is frequently so complex that one cannot achieve it by logic alone, at least not before the moment that it applies to has passed. Fortunately, that well-known high-speed illogical computer, the brain, can produce your answer in the form of an instinctive feel. Trust your instinct, even when your logic tells you that it must be wrong!

10 *Envoi*

New directions

The more I fish the more I realise how little I know. Boatfishing is a developing sport and the following areas are those in which there is considerable scope for any fisherman to advance the art.

No-one has yet succeeded in consistently taking fish very deep with insect imitations. Many of the larger brown trout I catch deep have been feeding on relatively small foodforms; shrimp, olive buzzer pupae, asellus and snails in the main. Despite considerable efforts on my part, my successes with natural imitations of these foodforms have been almost negligible. I am convinced however, that it must be possible; only time will tell.

Little is understood about the way in which trout will discriminate between one type or colour of lure and show a remarkable preference for a specific variation on certain days. Colour and size are certainly of crucial importance, less well understood are the factors that affect the action of a lure, particularly in producing vibrations when retrieved.

What is really required is for someone with much time, much tackle and access to a quiet swimming pool to carry out a series of experiments and find out just how a lure does work in the water. And, for that matter, to find out exactly what track a lure follows when fished in conjunction with a fast sinking line. Nobody really knows about that even now.

Vibration and flash-effect lures are at the seminal stage of development and offer major scope for taking deep-lying trout on bright windy days (provided, of course, they can be kept within the bounds of legality).

Imitating the natural insect is only in an early stage of development. No-one has yet satisfactorily explained the startling effectiveness of such flies as the Soldier Palmer or the White Wickham; nor has anyone worked out effective adult sedge imitations. The problems of the adult chironomid are even less well understood. Only Bob Carnill, the brilliant fly dresser, seems to have devoted time to making a proper study of that insect form.

On the technical side, no-one has produced a flyreel fit for using with a shooting head. We need a reel based on the Pflueger Medallist design with a drum 4½" in diameter, ½" wide, light-weight and durable, probably made out of a composite fibre and matrix material.

Pointing out gaps in knowledge may seem irrelevant to those who find the main business of catching fish by conventional methods difficult enough to accomplish. Ultimately, though, to some it becomes unsatisfying to catch fish by the repetition of known tactics in tried situations.

A large part of the pleasure of fishing lies in solving new problems as well as those that already exist, and even the newest beginner to the sport can make valuable contributions by running the right experiments. Obviously there are drawbacks because any real advance takes time, trouble and the conscious foregoing of more easily taken fish; these vanish into irrelevance as soon as one cracks a problem. The intellectual pleasures are phenomenal and one can be as high as a kite for days! One warning for would be pioneers: fly fishing literature is bedecked with discoverers of techniques, flies or whatever which are 'the answer'. Often 'the answer' subsequently catches no more than a handful of fish. If you think you have dis-covered something, test it thoroughly before you publish; you will look very foolish if you have generalised wrongly from a sample of one.

Protecting fisheries

It is all too easy for fisheries to be ruined by inept management, and I for one would not be unhappy to see Fishery Managers treated like Football Managers: two bad seasons and cheerio! The only way in which we can safeguard our sport against the excesses of some of the cranks that I have seen as Fishery Managers is the political way. We owe it to ourselves to organise rapidly and effectively; as a fly fishing Club Secretary I can confirm that Water Authorities take heed of organised fishermen, they respond well to reasoned suggestions and even more swiftly to an orchestrated campaign of protest. If you are unwilling to stand up and be counted then do not be surprised if pike and yachtsmen replace the trout in your favourite fishery.

In addition, considerable pleasure can be gained from Fishing

Clubs: both in and out of season. Lectures, films, expert tuition, friendly competitions or just extending the circle of friends and acquaintances. The main thing is to be involved, to take part and to help. Without Fishing Clubs there may be no Fisheries.

Fitness

Boatfishing is an exhausting business, few other sports occupy up to thirteen hours in a day. The ability to execute the physical and mental aspects effectively over such a long period does not come naturally, a considerable amount of training is required. I always ensure that I have had a number of fairly strenuous casting sessions in the months of January and February prior to the start. In addition, I recommend a couple of days fishing off the bank, not to catch fish particularly, but to refamiliarise oneself with the feel of the tackle in the hands. During a long layoff, the fine co-ordination required for effective retrieving and striking invariably suffers.

Boatfishing is a serious affair and nobody can hope to become competent without regular practice; at least one day per week is necessary to keep one's hand in.

There is no point in going fishing when you are physically unwell. Better far to give your partner plenty of advance warning and have a substitute available to take over from you. Over the years I have fished with flu, tonsilitis, gastric infections and glandular fever; no lasting physical harm resulted, but I hardly managed any real fishing at all and distracted my partners. If you are ill, stay in bed until you are better, don't take chances of making yourself worse by physically stressing yourself with a long day afloat.

Confidence

Confidence is a major factor; fishermen without confidence will catch very few fish. Often during the course of a day or a few weeks one will either get 'hot' or go into a slump often for no good reason. One frequent and identifiable cause of a slump is the tightening up that accompanies your partner's spectacular success. This tightening up ('choking' the Americans call it) applies to every sporting activity. As the confidence seeps away, so does the relaxed ease of good performance. In fishing the symptoms are retrieving too quickly, missing easy takes, and impatient behaviour.

Whenever your partner starts to get away from you, what you must do is to exaggerate the ease with which you are fishing and attempt to fish calmly, slowly and methodically. As soon as you can force yourself to relax and enjoy it you will nearly always start to catch fish again. Anyway, sooner or later, statistics will catch up with you. With two of you in a boat the odds on one of you catching a fish instead of the other are the same as the odds in tossing a penny to come up heads. The longest similar run I have ever heard of was 27 consecutive Reds turning up at roulette at Monte Carlo. If the run is against you there is nothing you can do about it except be patient and wait for the odds to swing your way; it just may not be your day.

The longer slump is harder to shake. I suffer from a long slump of maybe a month at least once a season. My ways out are to start serious experimenting; fishing for very difficult fish, pushing techniques to their limits; to have a day deliberately fishing for stockfish to restore the confidence by sheer weight of numbers, or to have a trip out to another water for a complete change of scene.

It is possible to lose your edge through intensive fishing. Over a season I reckon to put in about 40 boat trips and 60 bank trips, all on the same water. This can result in my being fished-out by mid-September. A sensible thing to do is to arrange a mid season break doing something different somewhere else. A word of warning though – the last two seasons I have been fortunate enough to have a week on the Dovey and boating pales when compared with night fishing on that river for seatrout; the following few trips to Rutland were rather an anticlimax.

Sportsmanship

It is worth remembering that the overall objective of the day is to maximise the pleasure of both occupants in the boat. Very often, it is possible for one fisherman to hog all the fishing by manipulating the boat or just by the luck of sitting in a particular seat. Whenever I fish I make a positive attempt to manoeuvre the boat in such a fashion as to give myself and my partner an equal chance of catching the fish. There is naturally an element of enlightened self-interest as I am well aware that a half share of the product of two fishermen fishing at 70 per cent effectiveness is greater than a half share in my operating at 100 per cent effectiveness and my partner catching nothing at all.

This principle has to be extended. Courtesy on the water costs little and a moment's thoughtlessness can ruin someone else's sport for half an hour. It is not easy to forecast exactly where a boat will drift but it is very easy to take the long way round and avoid disturbing the water downwind. It is equally easy to avoid disturbing bank fishermen.

Having fun

It is frequently said that one needs bad days to remind one how good the good days are. In some ways the bad days are in fact the best ones for they not only test the character but they provide an essential springboard: the frustration of defeat is the spur that makes one go back to the water with new optimism.

Any fool can enjoy the good days, it takes a real fisherman to enjoy the bad days, learn from them and cope with them better the next time.

Appendix I: Rods

I carry the following rods. Some overlap in their various functions in case of breakage.

SMALL FLY RODS

  (i)   10 foot Lamiglas Carbon Fibre AFTM 6/7.
 (ii)   11 foot Bob Church Carbon Loch Style AFTM 6/7.
(iii)   12 foot Fibatube Carbon Loch Style AFTM 5/6/7.
(iv)   15 foot Shakespeare Dapping Rod Serial 1081-465.

LURE RODS

 (i)   10½ foot Fibatube Carbon AFTM 8/9/10.
(ii)   10½ foot Fibatube Carbon AFTM 13 leadliner.

All the rods I recommend have the following notable features:

(1)   Minimum length 10 feet.
(2)   Ringed throughout with Fuji or Seymo rings to cut down on line wear.
(3)   Where feasible, all rods are Carbon fibre. Sensitivity is the paramount reason. All the rods above can be variously duplicated in glass; alas, they don't fish so well.
(4)   The buttring is positioned at the limit of a comfortable left hand reach.
(5)   Three 1" corks are fitted below the screw winch: enables the rod butt to be held against the stomach whilst playing a fish; cuts down the leverage on the wrist by the mass of the reel when casting.
(6)   All screw winches feature double locking rings set to lock up the rod not down. On my lure fishing rods the rings are at 90° to the reel. This assists fishing at the bow position in Northampton style..
      I hold the rod in a halfway position. It feels much more comfortable and does not affect the casting at all.
(7)   The overall length of the handle reaches from the elbow to one inch in front of my right forefinger. Grip thickness must be regulated to suit the individual, an over thick grip blocks the

wrist action, an over thin grip overemphasises it. I favour parallel and scroll handle profiles, the cigar profile is excellent for short range high accuracy casting, there is little call for it in boat fishing.

Appendix II: Casting

The best fishermen are often the best casters. In stillwater fishing in general and boatfishing in particular it is a great advantage to be able to cast long distances and have the ability to handle heavy equipment. This implies a reasonable degree of strength and a mastery of the double haul technique. A fisherman who cannot double-haul is like a runner with a wooden leg.

There are four specialised techniques to be mastered:

(1) Long distance shooting head casting downwind from a seated position. To execute correctly, this requires the backcast to be allowed to fall below the horizontal. The forecast must be aimed up about 15 degrees above the horizontal.

(2) The lead-cored shooting head, being very heavy indeed, requires a short casting sequence: a roll, a backlift and a delivery. It must be cast with a pronounced upward stroke, at much the same angle of attack that a javelin thrower uses, about 25 degrees above the horizontal.

   The leadcored shooting head sorts the men from the boys at casting; it also teaches tournament technique. If you can cast one 40 yards, think about joining the British Casting Association and making an alternative use of your skills.

(3) Shooting Head braking technique. In order to ensure that the leader lands fully extended, it is essential to acquire the habit of slowing the last few feet of the shoot. This is done by allowing the backing to run between the forefinger and thumb of the hauling hand and then gently braking the shoot by tightening the grip.

   A mastery of this technique allows one to fish accurately and at long range for rising fish. Aim to overcast the distance and brake the head at the tail of its flight. A major assistance is fluorescent monofilament which makes it easier to follow the line in flight.

(4) The fourth is to develop a backhand delivery using double haul. This is essential for the helm position fisherman in Northampton style. It is one safe way of casting in a severe wind; and can be used in casting competitions to the amazement of spectators and the impoverishment of parties who like to place wagers on apparently unlikely outcomes; yes, one *can* cast forty yards backwards.

Appendix III: Lines

I carry the following lines. I always have a spare one with me.

FLOATING LINES

(1) Cortland Gloline DT/AFTM 5.
(2) Cortland Gloline DT/AFTM 6.
(3) Garcia Longbelly FT/AFTM 7.
(4) Gladding Super Aerofloat Green AFTM 9 33 foot shooting head.

SINKING TIP

(1) Home–made from 6 yards from the belly of an AFTM 9 floater with 5 yards of tapered Wet Cel II AFTM 5 spliced to it – weight 260 grains.

SLOW SINKERS

(1) Garcia Slow Sink AFTM 9 – 33 foot shooting head.
(2) Wet Cel II AFTM 9 – 33 foot shooting head.

FAST SINKERS

(1) Wet Cel II AFTM 11 – 33 foot shooting head.
(2) Super Aquasink AFTM 9 – 36 foot shooting head.
(3) Canadian Lead Impregnated AFTM 10 – 33 foot shooting head.

LEADCORES

(1) Gladding Mark V 45 lb. – 30 foot shooting head.
(2) Cortland Kerboom AFTM 13 – 30 foot shooting head.

COMPOSITE LINES

(1) Long Wet Cel II – FT AFTM 10 spliced to another by the thin ends.
(2) Long Super Aquasinker – FT AFTM 9 spliced to another by the thin ends.

(3)   20 yards Gladding Mark V 45 lb. lead core looped to 75 yards of
      fine Super Aquasinker running line cut from three AFTM 6 FT
      lines.
(4)   Long Lead, 100 yards of Gladding Mark V 20 lb. BS leadcored
      trolling line.

I regard lines in the way that a golf player regards his clubs or a
shooter his guns, each will perform one function excellently and
other functions less well. It is a major advantage to carry as wide a
variety of lines as one can afford. In years to come when the manu-
facturers have finally been persuaded to adopt a common standard
for defining sinking rates of line on a logical basis, the fisherman will
be able to purchase a balanced set of sinking lines that will enable
him to cope with all situations.

Until then one can only work by trial and error and in this context
it must be noted that some lines obtain their weight by means of a
dense plastic coat, others by having a loaded core. Where the
coating is the medium carrying the weight, the higher the AFTM
number, the quicker the line will sink. An AFTM 10 Wet Cel II sinks
noticeably faster than an AFTM 8. With core loaded lines, the
reverse is the case: an AFTM 10 Super Aquasinker sinks noticeably
slower than an AFTM 6.

Hence it is not sufficient to buy a line by brand name alone, everything must match; the AFTM number is equally important. Lines
have mass as well as density and the performance in the field is
further affected by the nature of the backing and the construction of
the lure attached. Drag factors in fall have to be appreciated and
taken account of.

All my sinking lines and shooting heads have a loop sewn and
whipped onto either end. I attach backing and leader with the same
knot, a four turn four tucked half blood knot, with the tucks con-
tinued to match the turns. This system has advantages:

(1)   Backing can be changed very easily.
(2)   Shooting heads can be carried loose (although mine are not).
(3)   Lines can be changed on a rod by reeling in, changing the reels,
      cutting and retying the leader and then pulling the line through
      the rings; much quicker than by setting up another rod. (The
      leader must, of course, be longer than the rod.)

Appendix IV: Flies and lures

No fisherman worth his salt buys flies. The commercial fly is generally a pretty poor product constructed by non-fishermen in the Third World and sold to the gullible by tackle dealers who really should know better than to cripple local cottage industry. There are, of course, a few shining exceptions; Tom Saville in my area buys exclusively from high quality British professionals.

In a season I use, lose and give away upwards of a thousand flies. If I didn't tie my own I would find the odd few hundred pounds this represents hard to come by; besides, I tie the flies the way I want them with the right materials and decent hooks.

HOOKS

Good hooks are essential for success. I recommend Mustad and Partridge down-eyed lure hooks and only Partridge wide-gape down-eyed wetfly hooks; for heavy wire hooks use the Mustad 7780c. Buy hooks in hundreds and inspect at least two from each box. They should be tough without being brittle, short in the point, short in the barb and sharpenable.

Sharpen your hook before you use a fly in the following manner: work along one side of the hook with a flat carborundum stone, go from the bend to the point at a 45° angle. When you have worn a small flat repeat the procedure on the other side. Work back and forth until the finished product has a triangular profile at the point. The removal of metal has a weakening effect upon the hook. Hooks that are poorly tempered or have too deeply cut barbs may break behind the barb on the strike.

Messrs Fog distribute a diamond hook sharpener, the Eezi-lap. It has a triangular channel. Although expensive, it is the best sharpener on the market. I use one to finish my hooks.

TANDEM CONSTRUCTION

All that is required of a tandem rig is that the linkage is stronger than the leader. I use two linkages, both have to be subjected to a minimum of 25 lb. static load before they collapse; neither has ever broken on a fish.

The first linkage uses 40 lb. BS round-section monofil blobbed at each end with a flame. Use unwaxed silk so that varnish can penetrate through it, whip up and down each hook and varnish twice with clear nail varnish.

The second linkage is made from 35 lb. BS Seastrand plastic-coated stainless steel wire. This is used because it does not droop and can be bent slightly to ensure that the flying treble can be concealed in the hairwing. This rig was developed simultaneously and separately by Stewart Billam and Terry Griffiths. It is constructed as detailed:

(a) Put treble into vice, dab with Superglue, or Evostick; before the glue dries, rapidly whip the steel wire along the shank.
(b) Repeat the process on the front hook.
(c) There should be no need to varnish as the Superglue or Evostick can be very liberally applied.
(d) After dressing the front hook, angle the linkage to put the treble hook in the centre rear of the wing.

I also use this technique to wire two double hooks together on which I dress huge Mylar Bucktails, 4 to 6 inches long and double tandems for use against large browns.

TUBE FLIES

All tubes should be tied on Saville's no. 4 size clear plastic tubing. Method of dressing:

(1) Insert appropriate sized embroidery needle in vice.
(2) Slide tubing over needle, push until it jams and cut off ½" length.
(3) Select six identical appropriate hackles, strip the flue, tie onto tube.
(4) Turn the needle through 180°.
(5) Repeat with six identical hackles.
(6) Whip off.

It is essential that the wings are set like a very steep roof. Parallel set wings are no good.

All tube flies must be fitted with a clear plastic extension tube (Fig. 29). The length of the extension tubing can be varied depending on where you wish to position the hook. Extension tubing is obtainable from Saville's.

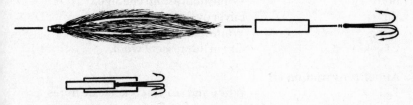

Fig. 29 Tube fly assembly showing position of extension tubing

SPECIAL FLIES

In addition to the large numbers of standard flies mentioned in the text I use a variety of other flies the dressings of which are listed below.

SINGLE AND DOUBLE HOOKED FLY DRESSINGS

White Rabbit nymph

Tail	– Thick, white rabbit body fur guard hairs.
Body	– Dubbed white rabbit underfur.
Rib	– Fine silver wire.

Flat Wing Missionary *R. Shrive*

Hook	– Standard shank length.
Tail	– Pale ginger cock hackle point set on flat (to act as a brake).
Body	– Fluorescent white chenille, wool or tow.
Rib	– Fine silver oval.
Hackle	– White, orange, scarlet or scarlet under white to suit your tastes.
Wing	– Silver mallard spoon shaped emergent pinfeather set on flat with curve over back of hook (to act as a parachute).

White/Orange

Hackle	– Hot orange cock.
Rib	– Silver oval.
Body	– White chenille.
Wing	– Arctic fox tail.

White/Green

Body	– White fluorescent chenille.
Rib	– Silver oval.
Wing	– White marabou.
Cheeks	– Green fluorescent wool.

Appetizer variation (1)

Tail	– White and scarlet cock hackle fibres mixed.
Body	– White fluorescent chenille.
Rib	– Fine silver oval.
Underwing	– White marabou.
Wing	– Grey squirrel.
Hackle	– Short scarlet cock, long white cock in front, raked back.

Appetizer variation (2)

As above substituting Peacock herl for grey squirrel.

Baby Doll variations

All are dressed fat and have painted eyes.

(1)	Green line	– Green fluorescent chenille along either side of back.
(2)	Fluorescent backs	– Green, orange and red.
(3)	All fluorescents	– All-green fluorescent, all-orange.

Zero

Hook	– 2/0 L/S, 4/0 L/S silver Aberdeen.
Tail	– Long scarlet dyed cock hackle fibre.
Body	– Heavy white chenille.
Rib	– Silver oval.
Wing	– Skunk tail – 3" long.
Hackle	– Scarlet & white cock wound together and raked back.

White Flectolite

Hook	– L/S 4 or 2.
Body	– White fluorescent chenille.
Rib	– Silver oval.
Hackle	– Hot orange.
Wing	– White goat or backtail.
Flanks	– Doubled wide strip of gold flectolite.

Black Lure

Body	– black chenille.
Rib	– Silver oval.
Hackle	– Black.
Wing	– Black dyed squirrel.

Bloody Maria

Body	– Strip of plastic leather, pearl silver colour or Mylar tube.
Hackle	– Scarlet.
Wing	– Black dyed squirrel.

John Player Special   *(D. Clark)*

Body	– Strip of bright gold plastic simulated leather or gold Mylar tubing.
Hackle	– Large black cock, raked well back.
Wing	– Black dyed squirrel.

Zuluka

Tail	– Crimson wool, variation with neon magenta wool.
Body	– Black chenille.
Rib	– Gold or silver oval.
Wing	– Six black cock hackles matuka dressed down the back as full feather. Do not strip the undersides.
Hackle	– Large black cock wound as a collar and raked back.

Murderer   *(R. Burgin)*

Tail	– Scarlet wool.
Body	– Black chenille.
Rib	– Wide silver tinsel.
Wing	– Black marabou.
Hackle	– Dyed scarlet cock.

Tadpole *(T. Griffiths)*

Hook	– Mustad 7780c 6,8,10 – leaded and unleaded
Tail	– Black marabou.

| Body | – Black and fluorescent green banded chenille, ribbed gold wire. |

Also all black, all orange and all white variations.

White Chenille Headed Lures *(G. Davis)*
Tail	– Cock hackle fibres.
Body	– White chenille.
Rib	– Silver oval.
Wing	– White marabou.
Head	– White chenille.

White & Green *(G. Davis)*
Tail	– Green fluorescent wool.
Body	– White chenille.
Rib	– Silver oval.
Wing	– White marabou.
Cheeks	– Green fluorescent wool.
Head	– White chenille.

Black
Hook	– LW Double 2,4,6.
Tail	– Long, black dyed squirrel.
Body	– Black chenille.
Rib	– Gold oval.
Wing	– Black marabou under, black squirrel over.
Head	– Black chenille.

Black & Green *(G. Davis)*
Tail	– Green fluorescent wool.
Body	– Black chenille.
Rib	– Gold oval.
Wing	– Black marabou.
Cheeks	– Green fluorescent wool.
Head	– Black chenille.

MUDDLER VARIATIONS

Minstrel *(D. Greaves)*
| Body | – Black floss. |
| Wing | – Black squirrel. |

Rib   – Close ribbed, silver oval.
Head   – White deer, spun and clipped.

Double ender
Tail   – Grey squirrel.
Body   – Rear third spun deer hair (Red Deer
                           preferably). Front two thirds copper
                           lurex ribbed copper wire.
Underwing   – Grey squirrel.
Wing   – Oak turkey tail.
Head   – Spun Red Deer fur, clipped back.

Ogston
Tail   – Long, grey squirrel.
Body   – Arc Chrome, signal green or neon
                           magenta floss.
Rib   – Flat silver tinsel.
Wing   – Mixture of black marabou, turkey,
                           pheasant centre tail fibres or anything
                           you fancy.
Head   – Roe Deer, spun and clipped.

Keetleys White   *(A. Keetley)*
Tail   – Short and thick, white marabou.
Body   – White fluorescent chenille.
Rib   – Gold or silver oval.
Wing   – White marabou, Arctic fox tail overwing.
Hackle   – Hot orange dyed cock hackle.
Head   – White dyed deer hair, spun and clipped.

Copper Flectolite
Underwing   – Grey squirrel.
Flash Wing   – Doubled copper flectolite cut to
                           willowleaf shape set on either side of
                           underwing.
Head   – Spun clipped Red Deer.

Green and White
Body   – ·Fluorescent green chenille.
Wing/Hackle   – White marabou or synthetic fur put on
                           evenly all round the hook.

Yellow Maroon Lure

Body	– Maroon chenille, ribbed gold or silver oval.
Hackle	– Pale sulphur yellow, large and raked well back.
Wing	– Six pale sulphur yellow cock hackles.

Squirrel and Green

Tail	– Bunch of fluorescent green dyed cock hackle fibres.
Body	– Fluorescent green chenille.
Rib	– Gold wire.
Wing	– Grey squirrel.
Hackle	– Fluorescent green dyed cock.

TANDEM LURES

Tandem Black

Bodies	– Black chenille.
Rib	– Silver oval.
Wings	– Black marabou, black dyed squirrel over.
Hackle	– Large black cock, front hook only.

Greenstripe Black

As above with green fluorescent wool cheeks extending half the hook length on the front hook only.

Black Christmas Tree

Tails	– 2 thicknesses neon magenta wool.
Body	– Black chenille.
Rib	– Silver oval.
Wing	– Black marabou.
Cheeks	– Green fluorescent wool.

White Christmas Tree

Tails	– 8 strands of arc chrome fluorescent floss.
Body	– White fluorescent chenille.
Rib	– Silver oval.
Wing	– White marabou.
Cheeks	– Green fluorescent wool.

White & Silver

Rear Hook – Tail	–	White marabou.
Body	–	White fluorescent chenille.
Wing	–	White marabou.
Front Hook – Tail	–	White marabou.
Body	–	Two thirds white fluorescent chenille.
Flash Wing	–	Long doubled strip silver flectolite.
Overwing	–	White marabou.
Head	–	White deer spun and clipped, large.

White and Gold

As above with flash wing of gold flectolite.

Black and Copper

As above substituting black for white; and copper flectolite flash wing. (Also useful tied with very long thin flash wings in a scorpion variation.)

Green Giant

Tails	–	Fluorescent green wool.
Bodies	–	Fluorescent green chenille, ribbed fine gold oval.
Wing	–	Fluorescent green marabou.
Hackles	–	Fluorescent green.

Red Baron

Tails	–	2 thicknesses neon magenta wool.
Body	–	Fluorescent red chenille.
Rib	–	Silver oval.
Wing	–	Scarlet marabou.
Cheeks	–	Green fluorescent wool.

Scorpion   *(S. Billam, T. Griffiths)*
(Front hook only)

Body	–	White fluorescent chenille or silver tinsel.
Hackle	–	White or hot orange cock.
Wing	–	White bucktail.

Mylar Bucktail (Black and Silver)

Hooks	–	4 to 2/0 Wilson L/W salmon doubles.

Rear Body	– After lashing wire to rear double, slide a tube of thick Mylar down wire to bend of hook, fray out ½″ and tie down.
Front Body	– Lash above assembly to front hook, tie down Mylar at rear.
Mid Wing	– Black bucktail tied sparsely in bunches down either side of rear Mylar body.
Front Body	– Slide Mylar tube down hook, secure at rear over mid wing roots. Secure at front.
Wing	– Black bucktail over all.

Brown, Yellow and Gold

As above, substituting gold Mylar for silver; wing: yellow bucktail under, brown over.

TANDEM VARIATIONS

Instead of using double hooks, a Scorpion rig consisting of a silver treble size 8 at the rear and a long shank size 2 at the front is more effective when fishing for rainbows.

TUBE FLIES

White	– 1¼–5 inches long.
Black	– 2–5 inches long.
Pale Yellow	– 2–3 inches long.
Hot Orange	– 2–3 inches long.

Greenstripe Variations on White and Black.

INSECT IMITATIONS

Buff Buzzer

Body	– Palest beige dyed swan (just off-white) herl.
Rib	– Fine gold wire.
Thorax	– Mid-beige dyed sealsfur (ginger pink)
Wingcases	– Body herl shell-backed over thorax.

Polypropylene Black Buzzer

Body	– Dubbed black polypropylene dubbing.
Rib	– Fine silver wire.
Thorax	– Dubbed black polypropylene.

Pheasant Stick – L/S 12, 14

Tail	– Phosphor yellow or arc chrome fluorescent wool, short.
Body	– Thin, cock pheasant centre tail fibres.
Rib	– Copper wire.
Hackle	– Four turns ginger henny cock, medium short.

Tobacco Sedge (Emergent)   *(A. Knight)*

Body	– Dark sienna sealsfur, taken well round the hook – thickened at thorax.
Rib	– Gold wire.
Wing	– Mallard secondary (grey) dressed double and short.
Hackle	– Ginger cock, sparse, straggly, raked well back.

Black Buzzer variation   *(A. Cove)*

Body	– Black tying thread taken well round the hook-bend.
Ribbing	– Four strands of electron white fluorescent floss twisted together in close spiral.
Thorax	– Peacock herl.

Sedge Pupa – 10 WG/12 WG   *(J. Sharp)*

Abdomen	– Dark green/olive dubbed sealsfur.
Rib	– Fine gold oval.
Thorax	– Hot orange seal (broken housebrick colour).
Wingcases	– Cinnamon coloured cock pheasant side tail fibres.
Hackle	– Hot orange dyed cock.

Buff Sedge Pupa   *(T. Saville)*

Tail	– Two ginger hen hackle points set flat in a vee.
Body	– Hare's ear.
Ribbing	– Gold tinsel.
Sidewings	– Cinnamon hen set in a vee profile, as long as the body.
Hackle	– Red game cock.

Turkey Green
Body	– Green Highlander seal's fur.
Rib	– Fine gold oval.
Hackle	– Red game, palmered.
Wing	– Oak turkey.

Sienna Sedge
Body	– Sienna seal's fur.
Rib	– Fine gold oval.
Hackle	– Red game, palmered.
Wing	– Cock pheasant secondary, reddish brown. Or Oak turkey.

SHRIMPS

Hare's Ear
Tail	– Protruding well round the hookbend – buff tipped hare's face guard hairs.
Rib	– Fine gold wire.
Body	– Pale ginger hare jaw fur mixed with hare's face fur. Dressed large, pale and carrot shaped. Better if picked out on the underside after ribbing.
Leading	– Can be leaded underneath.

Clement's Crustacean (*J. Clements*)
Tail	– G.P. Tippet fibres.
Body	– Hot orange dyed swan.
Rib	– Fine gold wire.
Hackle	– Long hot orange dyed cock, raked back flat along body.

= *Appendix V: The Drift Control Rudder* =

BILL OF MATERIALS

Bar	– ½" round section mild steel 45" long.
Bolts	– 18 off ⅛" diameter 1" long.
Nuts	– 36 off to assemble to bolt, ⅛" thick.
Plates	– 2 off 13"×9"×¹⁄₁₆" mild steel.
Front Blade	– Marine ply 13"×12"×½".
Rear Blade	– Marine ply 24"×18"×½".

OPERATIONS IN MANUFACTURING A RUDDER BLADE AND BAR

(1) Have somebody weld you one of the plates to the bar.
(2) Drill both plates clamped together to get the holes identical. Mine has 9 holes on either side of the bar.
(3) Loose assemble and mark out the trimming cuts on the blades.
(4) Trim the blades rounded and fine down the leading edge of the front blade.

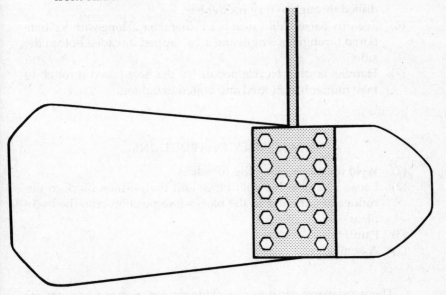

Fig. 30   Drift control rudder showing bolted plate

(5) Clamp each half blade in position onto fixed plate and drill.
(6) Varnish blades.
(7) Paint plates and bar.
(8) Assemble, saw off protruding bolts.

Locking Device

MATERIALS

(1) Steel plate $10'' \times 2'' \times 1/8''$.
(2) Steel plate $10'' \times 8'' \times 1/8''$.
(3) Split block – mild steel $1\frac{1}{2}'' \times 1\frac{1}{2}'' \times 2''$
     $\frac{1}{2}''$ diameter hole drilled through (to take the rudder bar)
     $\frac{1}{8}''$ slot
     $\frac{5}{8}''$ hole drilled through half the slot
     $\frac{1}{2}''$ drilled through other hole, tapped and threaded
(4) Locking by using a $\frac{1}{2}''$ bolt $1\frac{3}{8}''$ long pushed through the $\frac{5}{8}''$ hole and screwed into the bottom hole. Weld a piece of light bar onto the head of the bolt.
(5) Position block – mild steel $1\frac{1}{2}'' \times 1\frac{1}{2}'' \times 3/4''$ with $\frac{1}{2}''$ dia. hole drilled through to take rudder bar.
(6) Security barrel. Mild steel bar $1''$ diameter $2''$ long with $\frac{1}{2}''$ hole bored through its length and a $\frac{3}{8}''$ tapped threaded hole in the side.
(7) Handle, a scrap bicycle pedal, $\frac{1}{2}''$ dia hole bored through to take rudder bar. Slotted and bolted to tighten.

ASSEMBLY INSTRUCTIONS

(1) Weld the plates along the $10''$ edges.
(2) Loose assemble the split block and the position block to the rudder bar, then weld the blocks into position onto the backplate.
(3) Paint.
(4) Assemble.

There are many versions of locking device, as many as there are rudders. Use your initiative.

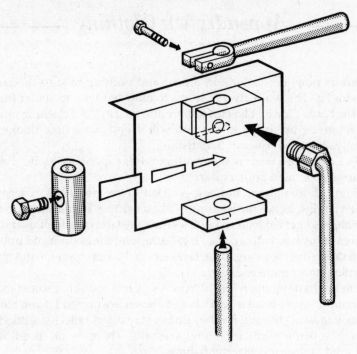

Fig. 31 Exploded assembly of locking device

Appendix VI: Clothing

There is nowhere to hide in a boat and nothing to stop the rain driving in. The wind always seems to blow harder and colder than on the bank. One just has to sit there and take it. Your clothing must therefore be up to the job or you will spend more time thinking grimly about the weather than fishing.

The clothing I wear is the result of bitter experience alone, I am contracted to no manufacturer.

Being short-sighted and bespectacled I have problems in seeing when it rains, hence the wearing of a baseball cap. In cold and windy conditions I get earache so I pull a knitted balaclava helmet over the crown of my baseball cap, fold it twice around the bottom and pull it well down over my ears. Balaclavas can be bought from most Army Surplus stores quite cheaply.

On bright days when forced to look towards the sun, I sometimes develop a severe headache. Polaroid glasses are no good if you have to look towards the sun for they do not stop direct reflected sunlight whereas plain, ordinary sunglasses do. There is no need for polaroid glasses in stillwater fishing.

A scarf, particularly a towelling one is a great advantage on wet or cold days. Coats are always a problem. I have a preference for Belstaff oilskin coats; they have a sensible two-way zip and the hood is integral. If yours has a detachable hood, Araldite it on by the studs and you'll never need to buy a replacement. The annoying feature of all oilskins is that the elbows and cuffs always wear out about three years before the rest of the coat. One day some manufacturer will reinforce oilskins on the undersides of the arms from the elbows down to the cuffs – then he will go rapidly bankrupt, no doubt.

Torrential rain requires an industrial quality rayon-backed PVC waterproof worn over the top of your oilskin.

A fishing waistcoat is a major advantage. I never fish without my Bob Church waistcoat. Its breast pockets house my scissors, forceps, stopwatch and several spare tins of mucilin are also tucked away in it – somewhere!

The upper body can be kept warm with sweaters. I prefer a combination consisting of a quilted waistcoat worn underneath a Javlin zip fronted fleecy windcheater. A long-sleeved shirt is an absolute necessity for sunny days; never take your shirt off in the boat unless you want a bad case of sunburn or are well-protected with sun-tan lotion. In severe heat you can keep cool by dipping your shirt in the oggin and then putting it on wet; the pleasure is absolutely animal.

Waterproof overtrousers are a necessity. I recommend oilskin ones which have a double thickness of oilskin across the seat. When it is warm rayon-backed plastic ones can be worn.

Next to the skin I wear corduroy or moleskin trousers. When it is freezing the ubiquitous Damart Thermal Underwear is a boon.

In the cold one can wear gloves but only if they are waterproof. Fingerless mittens are useful but protect the backs of the hands only.

Footwear should always be flat soled to prevent trapping the line. In warm weather I wear trainers; in the cold or wet, Derriboots. Do not wear waders, they are unsafe if you fall in and noisy if studded.

Every fisherman I have ever met knows more about appropriate clothing than his fellows so you will, no doubt, wear something else.

Appendix VII: Swivel Seat

MATERIALS

(1) Light ABS industrial chair.
(2) Two pieces of ⅛" plate, one 9"×6" the other cut to fit the chair base.
(3) 3½" of ⅞" diameter bar.
(4) 3¼" of ⅞" internal diameter tube.
(5) Four ¼"×1½" bolts with butterfly units to fit.

METHOD OF CONSTRUCTION

(1) Spark weld the bar to the 9"×6" plate, centrally. Drill four ¼" diameter holes, one in each corner, paint.
(2) Saw legs off chair, measure across support struts on base, cut second piece of ⅛" plate to appropriate size, tack weld to base supports of chair. Take chair off base support. Weld plate on fully, weld tube centrally to plate, reinforcing with bits of bar if necessary, paint and reassemble.
(3) The base is fitted to a seat plank by boring four holes in the plank in line with the hole locations and bolting through.
(4) To ease the swivel effect, counter bore the top of the bar to a depth of ³⁄₁₆" and a diameter of ⅜". Insert a ⅜" ball bearing and fix with superglue.

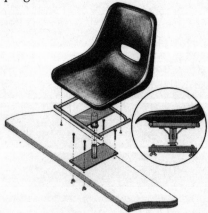

Fig. 32 Swivel seat

Index

66
666

Floatant 17
Floating lines 14, 16
Fluorescent backing 29
Fluorescent variation 79
Fly dressings 146–8
Flylines, deep fishing 37
Flylines, fluorescent 14
Flylines, Northampton style 59
Food populations 5
Footwear 153
Fry feeders 73
Fuller's earth 17
Fun 131

G-Cramp 12, 23, 36, 50
Game log 9
Ghillie 35
G.R.H.E. Nymph 20
Grappling iron 10
Grasshoppers – live 57
Gravid hens 105
Grease application 43
Greased, leader 21
Greased, sedge pupa 21
Greased, tip 19
Griffiths hatching buzzer 21

Hand twist 19, 42
Hatch representation 40
Hold on fishing 66
Hooks 137
Hotspot, cooling 23

Inconsistent fishing 2
Induced take 21, 45–6
Information net 122
Instinctive fishing 125–6

Jealousy 2
Jigging 118
Joke fly 22

Keel, hook 118
Keel, screwed 35
Knot, four turn 136

Lake Michigan 85
Landing net 13
Large floating flies 58
Largemouth Bass 87
Leadcore casting 134
Leader, anchor fishing 16
Leader, colour 28
Leader, cove dictat 16, 41

Leader, dapping 54, 58
Leader, deep fishing 27
Leader, extending 16, 32
Leader, flat calms 118
Leader, greasing 43
Leader, Long line 41, 42
Leader, Northampton style 65
Leader, tapered 16
Leader, variation 39
Leeboard 12, 50
Leech 5
Life jacket 112
Line burns 32, 75
Line burns, cure 32
Lines, sinking 31
Lines, standards 136
Line tray 113
Local knowledge 3
Longfall 74–5, 103
Longfall, flylines 75
Longlining 40, 45
Longlining, flylines 42
Longlining, rods 42
Longlining, subsurface 44
Long retrieve 74
Low pressure fishery 40
Lures, actions 78–9
Lures, anchor 23
Lures, dressings 78–9, 139–46
Lures, philosophy 77

Map, pre-flooding 4
Marrow scoop 5
Mayflies, live 57
Metred leadline 84
Micro climate 121
Microvariation 75, 125
Midwater nymph 20
Midwater, nymphing 20
Moonphase 4
Muddler and buzzer 48
Muddler fishing 47
Muddy waters 116
Multiplying reels 54

Natural insects 56–7
Necking loop 41
Netting drill 13
Night feeding 97
Noisy reels 82
Nymph reels 14
Nymph, rods 14